My Name Is America

The Journal of Scott Pendleton Collins

A World War II Soldier

BY WALTER DEAN MYERS

SCHOLASTIC INC.

New York Toronto London Auckland Sydney
Mexico City New Delhi Hong Kong Buenos Aires

England
1944

May 25, 1944

This journal was given to me by my uncle Richard, my mother's brother. He was the only one who gave me a gift at the going-away party my folks had for me. After the party Mom said that she didn't have anything to give me and I told her that I didn't need anything. I wanted to tell her about wanting my picture on the wall, but I didn't. Maybe when all of this is over I will tell her.

On the wall in the living room, over the settee, are two pictures. One of them is of my great-grandfather, Phillip R. Collins, who fought in the Civil War and was wounded at Second Manassas. In the picture he looks strong and proud and has eyes more or less like my father's, but he looks thinner than Dad. There is a Confederate flag in the lower center of the picture.

The next picture is of Dad, who was in the army during the First World War. He was stationed in Alabama and then went to France, where he served as an ambulance driver.

I would like to have my picture on that wall. It would

make me proud to show that I have served my country, just like my dad and great-grandfather did.

Bobby Joe Hunter came to our party and everybody toasted the two of us. Afterward I drove him home and we vowed that we would stick with each other no matter what. Me and Bobby Joe didn't get along too well in school. He's the kind of guy that always has to be the star of something. He played quarterback on the football team and I mostly sat on the bench. I heard from Jerry Villency that when Bobby Joe couldn't start on the baseball team, he quit. He's been pretty decent over here, so far, and we haven't had any trouble. When we reached England, we went on pass together and we traveled to a place called Stonehenge. It was really cold and rainy there. We were both glad to leave.

May 27

Today we had a long lecture about the Nazis and what they have been doing in Europe. After the lecture, which was really kind of boring, we saw a cartoon with Hitler and Tōjō, and that was pretty funny. Lt. Rowe said that the Germans were really good soldiers and were going to be tough to defeat. Bobby Joe said that the reason the Germans looked so good was because they hadn't fought Americans. I believe that Bobby Joe is right.

I wrote to Danny and Ellen, telling them what England looks like. A captain brought the letter back to me and said that I couldn't tell them where I was. He gave me the letter and I saw that he had crossed out everything except *Dear Danny and Ellen*, at the top; the part about us marching under the Admiralty Arch; and *Your loving brother, Scott*, at the end.

There are so many soldiers here in England it isn't funny. When we go over there, we'll probably have them outnumbered two to one.

We saw Eisenhower today. He was with two other generals. I was about fifty feet away and he looked like an all right kind of guy. As soon as he left we had to pack up and move again. This time we didn't just go to another camping area. The company commander said this was going to be the final staging site.

"I'm going to shoot about fifty Germans," Bobby Joe said. "But I want to bop one of them right in the nose."

That's Bobby Joe for you. Sometimes I think he would rather hit somebody than eat. But I also know that he is a serious guy. When I told him about this journal, he went back to his stuff and showed me what his folks had given him. It is a New Testament that his dad carried through the First World War. It has his dad's name, Gordon R. Hunter, written in the front.

"I'm giving it to my son when he goes in the army," Bobby Joe said.

May 28

It's spring but the weather is still chilly and damp. We're eating field rations and there aren't enough showers to go around. There was a rumor that we were going to go back to the main camp, but the captain says we're stuck here until the invasion starts. Everybody is ready. Bill Micu (we call him Mikey) says that the Germans are probably scared stiff. He says they're just sitting there looking over the water and thinking that they're not going to get back to *der Vaterland*, which means "the fatherland."

Jerry won $200 in a poker game and a whole mess of foreign money that we've all been given. I asked Sgt. Wilson why we were given the foreign money, and he said it was in case we ran out of bullets and had to buy some from the Germans. Ha ha.

Wojo and Mikey started calling me Smoothie because I don't shave. I don't care.

May 31

This morning we loaded up with all our gear and everybody thought this was going to be it. I was mad at Wojo because he said that there is nobody in Roanoke that can play ball with even the second-stringers from Winchester. That has got to be the most stupid thing I have ever heard in my whole life. Anyway, we got on the ship and sat around all day. I cleaned my M-1 and wiped some grease from the slide that I thought I had cleaned away before.

Sgt. Wilson was running his mouth as usual. He said that if we bayoneted a German in the chest and couldn't pull out the bayonet, we could get it out by firing a shot and pulling out the bayonet on the recoil. Bobby Joe said that if we could shoot the Kraut why were we fooling around with the bayonet in the first place? That made Sgt. Wilson mad. When they talk about the Germans they use names like Kraut and Jerry. Kraut comes from sauerkraut and I don't know where Jerry comes from.

I don't really mind what Wojo said about Winchester beating Roanoke but he didn't have to make so much of it.

Evening

We didn't go again but we went over the side of the ship, down the rope ladders, and into the assault boats for practice. The sea was choppy and Corp. Hubbard, Mr. Big Time from Charlestown, got sick before he got down into the assault boat. They call the boats LCVPs — Landing

Craft Vehicle Personnel. Dumb name, but that's the army for you. One of the navy guys said it was a Higgins boat.

Corp. Hubbard showed us a company flag that he is going to carry into France and put on the highest hill he can find. That made us all feel good. We're the best in the 116th Regiment and that's a fact! I don't think anybody in their right mind will say that I am wrong.

Got a letter from home. Dolph Camilli hit three home runs over the weekend. Angie Gardiner is looking for a part-time job and asked Dad for a recommendation. Mom said that Angie was talking about me a lot.

June 3

The rumor is that the Germans have killed Hitler and the war is almost over. I don't blame them. He sounds like a creep. Sometimes I have a dream about going into a building where there are a lot of Germans and seeing Hitler sitting at this long table. In the dream he goes for his gun but I level the M-1 and blow him away.

Mikey was talking about English girls being all hot to trot for American guys. He said he had to fight them off when he was in Picadilly. That's in London.

"They were trying to tear my clothes off," he said. "And one of them looked just like Hedy Lamarr."

If I had a girl that looked like Hedy Lamarr I would

marry her faster than you could blink an eye. Another girl I would marry RIGHT AWAY is Ann Miller.

There are two English girls working with the mess crew. Neither one of them looks like Hedy Lamarr, and neither of them is even as pretty as Angie, but I like the way they talk. Very proper.

Another rumor. The invasion has already started in Italy and the 101st Airborne has gone all the way through Italy and has attacked southern Germany. Any way they put it, we don't think there will be any big fighting until about a week after we hit France. Some guys from the 29th Infantry Division said that they saw orders for boats to start taking us back to the States by the end of October. I would like to see Paris before I go back. It'll probably be my only chance.

June 4

We loaded up again. We got off the boat again. Two guys from the DUKWs, which are armored vehicles that can go in the water, said that the 101st and 82nd Airborne had already landed and that they had taken 2,809 prisoners. They said some of the prisoners had had their eyelids cut off so they could not sleep, and all they could do was fight. The Germans must be desperate!

We all got letters from Gen. Eisenhower about us

going on the invasion. The letter was serious, about how the Germans would fight savagely and everything, but it made me feel good.

SUPREME HEADQUARTERS
ALLIED EXPEDITIONARY FORCE

June 6-1944

Soldiers, Sailors and Airmen of the Allied Expeditionary Force!

You are about to embark upon the Great Crusade, toward which we have striven these many months. The eyes of the world are upon you. The hopes and prayers of liberty-loving people everywhere march with you. In company with our brave Allies and brothers-in-arms on other Fronts, you will bring about the destruction of the German war machine, the elimination of Nazi tyranny over the oppressed peoples of Europe, and security for ourselves in a free world.

Your task will not be an easy one. Your enemy is well trained, well equipped and battle-hardened. He will fight savagely.

But this is the year 1944! Much has happened since the Nazi triumphs of 1940-41. The United Nations have inflicted upon the Germans great defeats, in open battle, man-to-man. Our air offensive has seriously reduced their strength in the air and their capacity to wage war on the ground. Our Home Fronts have given us an overwhelming superiority in weapons and munitions of war, and placed at our disposal great reserves of trained fighting men. The tide has turned! The free men of the world are marching together to Victory!

I have full confidence in your courage, devotion to duty and skill in battle. We will accept nothing less than full Victory!

Good Luck! And let us all beseech the blessing of Almighty God upon this great and noble undertaking.

Dwight Eisenhower

June 5

The dentist pulled a tooth from Sandy Froum. Right in the front, too.

We didn't go again. We got into the boats for practice anyway and went around in circles for a little while. I wish we could go back to Dartmouth. If Mikey was right about English girls being easy, I would like to find out about it. Wojo said that French girls were nasty. Sounds good to me.

Lt. Hanken asked me if I wanted to be the backup on the machine gun. I said yes but told him that I didn't know squat about the machine gun, except that it weighed a ton more than an M-1.

Later, on the ship

It's the middle of the night and we're on our way. I'm on *The Jefferson*, which is a good sign since that is the high school I went to. The chaplain had services. Some guys are playing cards. They should play with that funny money we got. That way if they lose it won't be so bad.

About an hour after we started out, the officers were going around saying that this was it, the real thing. Guys were cheering. I did, too, because I'm tired of waiting.

The English Channel is not that big but it's big enough. Some ships got there before we did and we could hear them open fire. If anybody didn't think this was the real thing, hearing those ships open up would make them think differently. We went up on deck and saw more ships than I have ever seen in one place at one time. Overhead there were these little blimp things. They call them barrage balloons. They are connected to the ships with steel cables, so that if planes come in low they'll get hooked up in the cables.

I feel myself getting nervous, like I'm about to play a big game or something, except I know this isn't going to be a game.

During the services the chaplain said that some of us wouldn't be coming back, and he offered up a prayer for our souls.

"If anything happens to me, will you take my Bible back home?" Bobby Joe asked me.

"Yeah, sure," I said. "And if anything happens to me, you can take this journal to my folks."

"Just make sure you write down the names of all the girls you know," Bobby Joe said.

Bobby Joe could not get to first base with any girl I know for two reasons. The first reason is that he talks about himself too much. The second reason is that he is not nearly as handsome as me.

Things are getting quiet on the ship as we get ready. I told Bobby Joe that if we got to Paris we could go around and look for girls and he said okay. Then he prayed. I prayed, too.

We were told for the first time what we are supposed to do. We are supposed to get on a beach called Omaha, take care of any Germans we find there, then follow the armored guys through this ravine to a place called Vierville-sur-Mer. Then we are supposed to hold that place until they get enough equipment onshore for us to move on. All the noncoms got to look at pictures so they would know just where the ravine is.

"There are five ways off the beach," Capt. Zappacosta said. "If we can't get off one way we'll find another. Either way we need to reorganize as soon as possible. We're going to fight in squads, platoons, and companies, just as we trained. Everybody got that?"

We all said yes. Capt. Z is a good man.

The section of beach we're going to is Omaha Dog Red. That's not the real name, but that's what we're calling it.

You can always smell the sea. On a good day it has the odor of faraway places. On this ship I can smell the sea but I can also smell the guys around me. Some of them are sweating. Some are breathing so hard you can hear it. We know we're going to be fighting and some guys are going to get wounded or even killed. That is what war is all about. I am a little scared myself.

I was going to write a letter to Mom but I didn't know what to write. I think I'll write to Angie, too.

June 7

If anybody finds this notebook, please send it to my father, Mr. James Collins, care of the Norfolk and Western Railway, Roanoke, Virginia.

I do not think I am going to make it through this fighting. It is too rough. When we came in I thought the whole world was falling apart. The sea was choppy and tossing everybody around, and some of the guys were throwing up. The noise was like the worst thunderstorm you had ever heard, but instead of being up in the sky it was all around you. It was more than all around, it was inside of us, shaking us. Me, Bobby Joe, Alonzo, Mikey, and Eddie Plummer were together in the assault boat. The boats formed a circle until they were all ready to hit the beach. My mouth went dry. Bobby Joe patted my arm and I took his hand and shook it. His hand was soaking wet.

I could see Omaha Beach through the smoke and haze as our assault boat rocked in the choppy waters. The noise was unbelievable — shells hissing overhead, great booms along the shore as the navy pounded the Nazi positions. Some of the guys were getting seasick and puking their guts out. A boat up ahead had been hit. Everywhere there were guys in the water. Some were splashing their way toward shore as the bullets kicked up the water around them. Others were already dead, their bodies floating against the steel obstacles. As we stopped on a sandbar, our boat's ramp dropped. I could hear fire from the automatics slamming into its steel sides.

"Okay, this is it! Everybody out! Let's go! Let's go!"

Somebody ahead of me screamed, and I saw his body go straight back and his arms fly into the air. There was a spray of blood and I knew he was hit bad.

An officer was yelling for them to keep the boat straight, and I saw the guys in front crouching down and moving forward into the water.

"Out of the boat! Out of the boat!" somebody yelled as more guys were getting hit.

I didn't know how he meant for me to get out because I was standing so far in the back. I climbed over the side of the boat and I was scared, I can tell you that. I thought we were closer in to shore, but we weren't, and I sank down under the water. I was scared and ashamed of being so scared and wanted to get back around with the other guys. The water was about four feet deep and I got to my feet and pushed hard to get to the front of the boat. When I got there, I saw that the guys had been shot up terrible. A shock went through me.

"Get to the beach!"

I heard a voice to my right and saw an officer trying to get men from another boat to the shore. The boat they were in was on fire.

Everything was in a panic. I turned and kept going to the beach. It looked a thousand miles away. The water was halfway up my thighs and getting in my boots and the sand was slipping out from under my feet. I could see guys falling, and I didn't know if they were shot or just falling. I saw other guys get hit — I knew they were shot by the way they jerked when the bullets hit them. One guy was cut nearly in half. His mouth gaped open as he twisted. I saw his eyes staring straight up as he fell backward into the water.

I was moving as fast as I could. They had these iron things sticking out of the water and some guys were down behind one, kind of crouched together, and I wanted to get there with them, but just as I started over one of them got hit. Half his face just blew away.

Half-stumbling, half-running over people and in a half-blind frenzy, I finally felt my legs out of the water. I was on the beach. I fell and when I did, bullets hit the sand right in front of me. Somebody grabbed my shirt and pulled me to my feet and we started running toward the wall, but whoever it was who helped me didn't make it. He went backward and I stopped for a minute to look at him. No, it wasn't a minute, it wasn't even a second, because when he went back some more bullets hit him and he slid sideways and I turned and ran up on the beach. I saw some guys huddled against a wall and I ran toward them.

I got to the wall where some other guys were and we just turned and looked back on where we had been. There were guys laying all over the beach. Most were still, but some were just wounded and trying to crawl away. There were guys in the water struggling to get out. There were guys just floating.

I can't write any more right now.

June 8

This is the second day since we landed. Nothing could ever be like the first day. Officers kept trying to get us organized and a lot of them were killed. I didn't see anybody from my company and I didn't know if they were alive or dead.

Guys were dying all over the beach. The seawall, which was about four feet from where I was, gave us some protection from the machine guns firing down on us, but not from the flanks. The only reason we weren't all dead is because more and more men kept coming in and the Germans were trying to kill them before they got out of the water.

I could see a gun sticking out from up on the small hill overlooking the beach, but there was nothing to shoot at, not with an M-1. An officer was walking up and down yelling at us to get up and going.

"You're either going to get off this beach or you're going to die here!" he was screaming.

Some guys had lost their weapons and they had to run back to the beach and pick up one from one of the dead guys. They dragged a few wounded under the seawall where the rest of us were crouched. But then a few guys started moving out, and I moved with them. We were out in the open again. There were brushfires off to my left as I headed toward the small hill in front of me.

The navy guns opened up again and I could hear the shells going over my head. The ground was shaking all around me.

"29 let's go! 29 let's go!" The guy yelling was running almost straight up. When he got hit and went down, guys just went past him.

The noise was so terrible. I wanted to shut it out but knew I couldn't. Some guys started climbing up to the next level of the seawall and I followed. We got to a gully that was filled with barbed wire. It was snarled and twisted, so there wasn't any use in trying to cut it. A sergeant pushed a bangalore torpedo through the wire. It went a little way and then got stuck. A lieutenant tried to push it farther into the gully, but he was hit. You could see where the bullets had ripped into his jacket. His body was shaking, but he got up and climbed onto the wire and kept on pushing the torpedo and got it clear. Then he died. The sergeant pulled his body away and then attached another torpedo to the first. We fired at anything that didn't look natural as we waited for the torpedoes to go off.

A burst of machine-gun fire went through the barbed wire, sending up a spray of sparks and dirt, and we all crouched down quick. I had my face in the sand when the torpedoes went off.

Somehow we were off the beach and pushing up the hill. When we got up the hill, we could see the guns from the German pillbox firing down onto the beach. I was on my belly and firing at what looked like a house over to one side. There was so much smoke, it was hard to tell what you were shooting at, but the kick of the rifle made me feel good, made me feel like I was fighting back. Back in training at Camp A.P. Hill, I was big on telling everybody how I could squeeze off a shot so smooth. Here I was shooting as fast as I could. No matter what I told myself, I couldn't calm down.

The rangers broke through first, and by about two o'clock I was on the hill overlooking the beach. The same general that was trying to get us up from the seawall was trying to figure out where the gulley was that we were supposed to go through. One of the pillboxes was still being held by the Germans, and a captain was calling for a flamethrower. I was crouched down and looked back over the beach and channel. It was awesome. There were wrecks all over the place, boats and tanks just off the beach looking like monsters reaching out of the sea. Things had quieted down to a point, enough so that they were trying to gather up the dead. On one side there were bodies floating in the shallow water. From where I was, I could see them bobbing in the current. There were so many dead guys down there. So many.

The last thing I wanted to do was cry, but I couldn't help it. The tears came and came.

"You okay, soldier?" an officer asked me.

"Yeah, I'm okay," I told him.

"You're a hero, son," he said. "You made it this far."

Out in the channel were thousands of ships. In the air over them were the barrage balloons. I looked at all of it, the ships, the balloons, the men crawling up the side of the seawall. I heard the *boom-boom* of the big guns, the constant rattle of machine guns, and the *chok! chok!* of a German gun in the distance. I threw up.

June 9

The hardest thing to do is to walk past the dead. Sometimes I want to look away from them, and sometimes I have to look. Looking at some soldier lying on the ground, his arms stretched out like he is just shielding his eyes from the sun, fills me with sorrow and fear. I know that if I am killed I will lie there like that until somebody comes along with a blanket to cover me, until somebody can take a dog tag and write down my name and serial number, until somebody carries me down to the beach to be taken home.

When I see somebody I know, or think I know, it is like a stomachache; the pain makes me want to turn and twist. So many from the 116th. So many. They said that A Company was nearly wiped out. Most of the guys in A Company were from Bedford and Roanoke. God, how sad it will be when the news gets home.

I saw my first German face-to-face today. He was a noncom and he was wounded pretty bad on his right shoulder, near his neck. A medic put sulfa on it and a bandage. Three of our guys watched and he kept watching us.

I think he thought we were going to kill him. I couldn't take my eyes off him. He was a Nazi. I wanted to see if he looked different from Americans. He didn't.

The thought came to me that he might have been shooting at me. He might have aimed at me and just missed.

"Did you shoot at me?" I asked.

He said something in German and shrugged. When he moved his shoulder he winced.

We got rounded up and an officer asked us what outfits we were in. When I told him I was with the 116th he pointed out a place up the road where he thought some other 116th guys were forming up.

"Look out for snipers," he said.

I found the other 116th guys, and the sergeant told me we were going to reform as D Company. He said to grab a bite to eat and get some rest, because we were moving out as soon as the company commander got back from a briefing.

A mess truck had been moved off the beach, and we had mashed potatoes, corn, and sliced chicken. As I ate I saw more German soldiers being brought in as prisoners. They were carrying their own wounded. Some smoked cigarettes.

Tired is mostly what I felt.

Next thing I knew they were organizing us into companies and this bigheaded sergeant was yelling at us.

"On your feet! I'm Sgt. Bunch. We're moving to a second objective. It's a seaside resort. You'll love it," he said.

We formed up and spread out and started our march into France.

June 10

All night I was numb. I don't think I dreamed. I don't know if I even went to sleep. Just dozed off once in a while. When I looked around I saw the other guys around me and they looked in bad shape. A medic went around looking for wounded guys. There were soldiers who had been hit and didn't know it. I don't understand that. Some of the wounds are terrible. A ranger had the lower half of his face smashed up. His jaw was twisted and where the flesh had been blown away, there was a dark clot of dried blood. He still wore his helmet, his eyes dark and shining from under the steel rim.

A major was going around trying to get the companies straight.

"We've got the Germans backing up so fast they're falling over each other!" he said.

All around me, I see men — either dead or wounded —

lying on stretchers or on the ground. If this is what it takes to make them back up, we've got a big problem.

"We're going to veer south from Vierville-sur-Mer," the major said. "Right here."

He tapped the map with a short, stubby finger.

A couple of guys looked over his shoulder and I did, too. Vierville was just a dot on the map. The new place he was pointing to was just dots and lines. I figured some German officer was doing the same thing with his maps. They would be waiting for us.

In the background there is always the sound of firing. Sometimes it is big guns, sometimes machine guns. Back in training I had a problem telling the difference between German guns and American guns. Here, I don't.

A major, his name is Bowie, or maybe Howie, told us he was going to get us a hot meal. I wasn't hungry.

Bobby Joe found me. God, I was glad to see him. He started talking to me about how his backpack had got shot up pretty bad. At first I couldn't even answer him.

"You doing all right?" he asked me.

"What kind of bullet did you take out of your backpack?" I asked.

He hadn't taken anything out of it and we went through it and found three ugly-looking pieces of lead.

"If I'd known I was that close to getting it I would have messed my pants," Bobby Joe said.

24

I told him I was afraid to check my backpack.

Bobby Joe started writing a letter to let his folks know he is alive. I feel discouraged and sad and alone as I sit here with all of these men around me, because now I know for sure that some of us are going to get killed. There's no question about it. I don't know why I'm alive now.

We're supposed to move out at daybreak. I'm so tired I don't want to move. When they tell us to get up from where we are lying, I just hope I can find the strength.

I am going to write down a copy of the letter I sent home. Just in case the real letter doesn't make it.

Dear Mom,

I am in Normandy. I can't tell you where. I am not wounded. We're doing all right so far. The Germans don't look like they're ready to give up, that's for sure. I've seen several French houses and a church. The houses are pockmarked from where shells have hit them. The church had only part of a steeple. There are civilians right here in the middle of this war. It doesn't seem fair. There are men, women, and children. The medics bandaged up a little girl today. She was about three, with dark brown hair and blue-gray eyes. Her leg was burned and her face was swollen real bad on one side.

Mom, I keep thinking about what the war would be

like if it was in Roanoke instead of here in France. It makes me almost choke up when I think about people in Roanoke, you and Dad and Danny and Ellen, having to worry about Nazis the way these people do.

One thing I wanted to tell you and Dad is that I love you both very much. Please tell Danny and Ellen that I love them, too.

Your son,
Scott

June 12

I have been over here forever.

Early this afternoon we were attacked by a German patrol. We were making our way from field to field at about two o'clock and got a little careless, I guess. The fields are separated by hedgerows. More or less they're just giant hedges that have been allowed to grow a long time without being cut back, so that the stems going into the ground are three or four inches thick. It's murder trying to get through them. The fields in Normandy go on forever, but they are not owned by one person or family. Instead they are divided up into smaller fields according to who owns them.

Anyway, we were trying to get through some hedgerows when we were attacked by a German company. They made a mistake, too, because they didn't know how many guys they were facing. Two of our guys got hit right away. As far as I could tell the Germans were not more than a hundred yards away, but they were on slightly higher ground than we were. I was one of the first to answer fire and I think I got the guy I was aiming at. He spun and his rifle spun, too, before it went out of his hands. They only got off one mortar round before our guys started laying down a blanket of fire. They threw a bunch of grenades at us, and we dug in close to the hedgerows. When they started moving out, we gave them enough respect to let them clear out before we moved up.

We got to the hedgerows and there were nine German soldiers wounded and two killed. I looked at the guy I thought I had shot. He was laying on his back looking like he was just taking a nap. It made me feel bad to think I had killed a man, but not as bad as I thought it would.

We took the weapons from the wounded soldiers and left them for the battalion medics.

We pushed down toward the Elle River. My left ankle hurt, and I asked a medic if he had anything to tape it up with. He said no, but gave me some APC tablets, which are aspirins. I asked him how he was doing. I didn't mean anything by it, it was just something to say.

The medic looked at me and shook his head. "If they're not hurt bad I don't do much," he said. "If they're hurt bad I don't do much, either."

I saw him helping a guy before. He was working hard to save him. I hope if I get hit he's around to help me.

We got to a place where we could see the river and were looking for a place to camp down for the night, when we started getting incoming artillery fire. I jumped into a ditch by the side of the road. There was water in the ditch, but I wasn't worried about getting wet. There was a sign on the road with an arrow that pointed in the direction we had been heading. It said St. Clair sur l'Elle. I keep reading these signs, wondering which town I'm going to die in. I don't want to think like that, but the thoughts come anyway.

"Three Squad! Move out!" The captain was pointing down the road, then curved his motion showing that Three Squad was going to move in from the left. Then he called out what One Squad and Two Squad were supposed to do. I forgot what squad I was in, so I went after Two Squad. Heads down, we ran along what looked like a cow path.

An old French woman was in one of the windows pointing at a two-story building with a steep roof. The shutters were green with white trim. They were closed. I looked around and saw that most of the windows had their shutters open. I aimed and shot through the shutters.

All the shutters opened and the Germans were firing back something furious. Some guys from One Squad saw what was happening and shot a couple of rifle grenades at the building. It was 10 minutes of heavy firing into the windows before we saw a white flag waving in front of one of them.

"Watch it!" the sergeant said.

We waited and after a while the door opened and a mess of Germans came out. I found out later that twenty-three came out with that crew. A lieutenant asked Brown, who speaks German, to question the prisoners.

The German officer's arm was already in a sling. He licked his lips before he spoke. Brown said that the officer told him there were three more Germans in the building.

"They're scared to come out," Brown said.

Which meant that somebody had to go in after them. All the other prisoners were made to sit out in the open while Three Squad went in. If they started firing from the windows again, they would hit their own men.

We waited for a while and we could hear our guys trying to get the Germans to give up. Then we heard shots and we got out of the clearing. One of the Germans who had given up tried to get up and move, and he was shot. I don't think he was trying to do anything, he was just scared. We zeroed in on the building, but shortly after that, our guys came out. They were okay. They didn't bring out any Germans and I didn't ask them what had happened in the house.

The Germans were knocked around a bit by our guys, but it wasn't too bad on them, just some bruises.

We dug in a little way from the Elle River. We had K rations and the guys who smoked lit up. I checked my gear and picked up some more ammo and some sulfa from the supply truck.

"You hurt?" It was the medic from before.

"No," I said. I was pissed at him for asking. I didn't want him to know that I was expecting to be hit any minute.

"Anybody got a map?" a tech sergeant asked.

I laid down and tried to get some sleep. Somebody had a radio with an English-speaking station. Not American-speaking, *English*-speaking, but they were talking about America. They thought some guy named Dewey was going to run against Roosevelt. I hope Roosevelt wins.

June 13

Early morning. It doesn't seem cold but my hands are shaking. Before we started off for the beach at Normandy,

I was excited and a little scared. I didn't know at the time what I was facing. Now, whenever we jump off to another battle, I am scared out of my mind. Today we're supposed to start to someplace called Couvains. The camp is quiet. It is also filled with smells. There is the smell of eggs and bacon cooking, the smell of the water we wash our mess kits in, and from somewhere, the smell of explosives drifts over us. There's not a lot of talking going on. I guess there's not a lot that anybody has to say.

We had a prayer service last night. The chaplain gathered all the guys who wanted to be there and we all either sat or knelt around the jeep he was using. The first prayer he started told everything about what was going on.

"Oh, Lord, look upon us this evening. . . ." Then he raised his head, looked at us, and said, "Don't bunch, guys."

He didn't want us to bunch up too close in case the Jerries sent in some artillery fire.

When the chaplain prayed for the dead, it touched us all. We had come over as an outfit of neighbors. Now there were spaces in our minds where friends used to be. I haven't wanted to write about the guys I was buddying around with before we hit the beach. I didn't even want to think about them. I knew Tommy Ward and Jerry Villency from back home. Tommy and I picked apples for a summer outside of Winchester. It was hard work, didn't pay much, but it was fun. I went to Jefferson High with Jerry.

We were going to double date if we ever managed to get dates. When we landed in Normandy, all the guys had been in the boat with me. I haven't seen any of them since.

Bill Darden and Dave Ewing I met at Camp A.P. Hill and we became pretty good friends. We hung out in the dayroom when we were in England, too, playing pool, whatever. Dave played the piano pretty good. He didn't know a lot of tunes by heart, but he could play "The Glow Worm" really good and also "Don't Sit Under the Apple Tree." That's the kind of song he liked. Bill, Dave, and I all agreed to go see *This Is the Army* when we got back to England and had a chance to get to London. I think Dave was from Bedford.

Another guy I sort of knew was Ellison. Back on D-Day, when I had made it to the wall, I looked back and I saw a guy I was pretty sure was Ellison. He had just reached the water's edge and was trying to crawl toward us. He had been hit already, and you could see the pain in his face. It was terrible and fascinating at the same time. We were all hoping he would make it, but none of us thought he would, and it was really like waiting for him to get nailed. When he got hit he just fell forward.

Sometimes it makes me feel guilty just being alive.

June 13, night

Couvains. I almost bought it today. The 115th was on the line and then they pulled back and we moved up. They made a path and we went right through them. They looked pitiful. Guys had bandages around their heads, around their arms and legs. And bodies. So many bodies.

"You think we'll ever get used to the killing?" I asked Bobby Joe.

"I don't know," he answered. "I hope it's over before we do. I don't want to get used to it."

We stopped on the edge of the city while the First Battalion got into position. Me and Bobby Joe got put into a new squad. They look like they're okay guys. They told me they had lost five guys from their old squad. Half the squad. I wished they hadn't told me that.

We were moving along the road when all of a sudden we're being fired on by the Germans. I guess I had been day-dreaming for a minute. It was like half daydreaming and half night dreaming. What's really going on is that I'm so tired I can't even think straight most of the time. I'm doing stuff more because I was trained to than anything else.

The captain was telling us to watch out for mines, so I was walking with my head down. Anyway, we got fired on and we ran into some buildings, which was scary by itself because you never know if there are Germans in there waiting for you.

The building I ran into was a warehouse of some kind. When I saw the people in it, I fired.

The guy started yelling something like Mayday. Another soldier came into the room and dove to the floor. I saw the old man clearly now. He was sixty, maybe seventy. So were the woman and the priest who flattened themselves against the wall.

I had my rifle pointed at them, and they stared at it. Then the old woman raised her hand like she was greeting me and I calmed down a little. McCormack, a guy I just met from Martinsburg, West Virginia, was the guy who had come into the house with me. We checked out the place real quick to make sure it was safe.

We didn't know how many Germans were out there. Through the window I saw a squad of men edging toward where the shooting had come from. Then the shelling began.

You could hear the German shells coming in and they were coming in fast. When they hit, I was ducking and trying to get under something. If a shell actually hit close enough to me I wouldn't have stood a chance of living. Anyway, when you hear the *boom* it means that the shell missed you and you don't have to duck. Nothing I could do but sit there with the three old French people and McCormack and take it.

The shelling went on and on. When shells hit close by, the building shook and parts of the wall crumbled. I wanted to shoot back, but there was nothing to see to shoot at. I just kept my head down as much as possible.

Once, when I looked up, I saw that the old people hadn't taken shelter. The guy was sitting on a wooden chair, kind of hunched over into himself, and rocking back and forth. The priest had his hands folded across his chest and his head bowed. The woman was peeling an onion. She was small and wrinkled with dark black eyes. The shelling, even when it missed, shook the earth and sent small wisps of dust into the air. It was through the dust and sunlight that I was looking at her when she smiled. I thought that maybe she had once been a young and beautiful woman.

"I think they're afraid to get down," McCormack said.

I looked at them, and motioned for them to get on the ground. The priest flattened himself at once but the old man went to the woman and helped her down first.

After what seemed like forever we got the word to move out toward the main part of town. The shells were still coming in, but we were moving out anyway.

"They've got this place zeroed in!" a lieutenant said.

We ran in groups of two and three back to where we had come from. There wasn't any small-arms fire. When I got back to the road there were two dead guys lying in the middle of it.

We crept in toward Couvains. Our artillery was sending in a barrage of fire, and you could see the smoke building up. When the artillery stopped, we started into the city again. By noon the fight was over.

Me and Bobby Joe and two other guys were assigned to guard some wounded Germans. The Germans looked terrible. One had a huge wound in his side, and he kept his hand over it. One had a head wound, and he was moaning and shaking. Our medics took care of our guys first.

Bobby Joe gave one of the wounded Germans a cigarette and he took it and just stared at it.

"It's a Chesterfield," Bobby Joe said.

The German's hands were shaking when he lit the cigarette. I thought he was just scared, but it must have been his wounds. He took a few deep puffs, then fell over dead.

I found out later that there wasn't any way of getting the Germans back safely. We couldn't afford the men. I asked an officer if we were going to let them go. He didn't say anything, just looked away.

McCormack is okay, only maybe not too smart. He says he's got a girlfriend in Roanoke who teaches school.

I think he wants to buddy up with me and Bobby Joe. He looks like a good soldier.

June 14

We're on reserve. The captain says not to get too frisky because the Germans don't know we're on reserve. McCormack said he'd send them a telegram.

I had bugs in my socks and a tick under my skin. McCormack burned it out with a cigarette. I took my first bath in Normandy. Actually, I took two baths. First, I got my steel pot filled with hot water and washed everything from my waist up because I was kind of nervous about taking my pants off in case we got shelled. The water felt so good I went back and got another pot of water and washed from my waist down.

"You getting to be a real pretty boy," Crockett said.

Crockett is from Wheeling, West Virginia. He's a big guy with half his teeth missing. He has false teeth, but he only wears them once in a while. He works in supply. I was thinking about how much I liked him and was wondering why. Then I realized that he's left over from the guys that I trained with back in the States. I don't know how many of us are left. I don't want to know.

I slept for almost nine hours. I had bad dreams that I don't want to write about now. Maybe later.

June 15

Crap. My squad has to go back to pick up some replace-ments. I swear somebody must have volunteered us. I asked McCormack, but he swears up and down that it wasn't him. The new guys are back in St. Clair. We took off at 0500 and reached St. Clair by 0730. Traveling with a squad instead of the platoon or even a company is scary. I keep thinking about how many Germans there might be around. Never, in all my life, do I think I'll get to be brave.

The guys we picked up are radio operators. One of them is a big-mouth gung-ho dude named Hightower, just out of Fort Gordon Signal School down in Georgia. He thinks he knows everything but he hasn't been in any fights yet.

"Where Hitler made his big mistake," Hightower said, "was when he thought he could walk over the United States the way he walked over Poland and the Nether-lands."

Then he went on about how the Nazis have taken over all these countries in Europe and how they think they are the master race and all. It all sounded like stuff you hear back home on the newsreels. As a matter of fact, Hightower reminds me of that chicken that comes on when they start the news.

When we got back to camp we had our first mail call,

but I didn't get anything. I don't know how they expect to find me when I've been in about three different companies in the last week. By the time you get settled in one company, it could be so chewed up they have to reform you into another company. Let Hightower deal with that.

Dear Mom,

I read in the papers (from Ohio) that Dolph Camilli is probably going to win the slugging award for the year. I think Uncle Richie has his autograph, but I'm not sure. Tell Danny to ask him about it.

I also read a lot of stuff about how the Russians are attacking Hitler on the eastern front. I hope that we are the ones who get him in the end. That will make all the sacrifices worthwhile.

I am doing fine so far. Fine means something different over here than it does in Roanoke, though.

There are plenty of rumors going around. One is that we have only three more objectives and then we get to go home. That makes sense to me. I don't know if you got my last letter. Do you think it would be all right for me to write to Angie? I have her address in my book (my little black book, ha ha) but I don't want to write to her if she is seeing somebody steady.

Your son,
Scott

June 16

Mail call. Some guy from the adjutant general's office came around and told everybody to destroy their letters after they read them. Two guys told him to take a flying leap. Right to his face. He started explaining that it was in case we got captured. I knew he wouldn't like me carrying around this notebook, writing down everything that's happening to me. But sometimes I feel that this is the only thing I have to leave behind. Some guys worry about their wives and children and here I am wishing I had a wife and some children.

We are still near Couvains. We're massing for an attack. My stomach feels queasy. I know it's because I am scared out of my mind. All I can think about is the day we landed. I told Bobby Joe and he came out with this big grin and I felt bad having told him that I was scared.

"Scotty," he said, "I'm so scared that if I ran right into myself I'd shoot me two or three times before I said hello. Only thing that keeps me from running is I don't know which way to run and I'm too tired to get up and look around."

I'm bone tired, too. Sleep over here is different than even back in England. I dream about dead guys looking up at me, hoping I'll do something, hoping I'll give them a hand and get them up on their feet.

Lt. Rowe is leading my platoon. He's a little over six feet and thin. I remember him being a good ballplayer back in Virginia and a pretty fair guy. He said nothing can be as bad as what we've already been through. Maybe. My mind says that what he says is true but I didn't know how it was going to be then. I know now.

A plane came by and dropped some leaflets. Some flew toward us and we got a few of them. They were in German, and somebody said they were leaflets we were dropping to tell the Germans to surrender. I hope the Germans listen.

(Supreme Headquarters, Allied Expeditionary Force)

BEKANNTMACHUNG

1. In dem unter meinem Oberkommando stehenden Kriegsschauplatz wird hiermit eine Militärregierung für die besetzten deutschen Gebiete errichtet. Die Militärregierung verfügt über die Vollmachten für Verwaltung sowie Gesetzgebung und Rechtssprechung, die in meiner Person als Oberbefehlshaber der Alliierten Streitkräfte und Militär-Gouverneur vereinigt sind.

2. Die erste Aufgabe der Militärregierung während des Fortgangs militärischer Operationen wird es sein, die rückwärtigen Verbindungen der alliierten Heere sicherzustellen und rücksichtslos alle Umtriebe in den besetzten Gebieten zu unterdrücken, die der baldigen Beendigung des Krieges entgegenwirken.

3. Zugleich wird die Militärregierung die Ausrottung des nationalsozialistischen Systems in Angriff nehmen. Die Militärregierung wird alle Mitglieder der NSDAP und der SS von verantwortlichen Stellen entfernen, ebenso andere Personen, die an führender Stelle am nationalsozialistischen System beteiligt sind. Diese Schritte werden sofort nach Eintreffen der alliierten Armeen und Einsetzung der Militärregierung in Angriff genommen.

4. Die Zivilbevölkerung hat nach Möglichkeit ihren normalen Beschäftigungen nachzugehen. Eingehende Bestimmungen werden für sie von den zuständigen Militärbehörden jedes betreffenden Gebietes erlassen werden.

DWIGHT D. EISENHOWER
General,
Oberster Befehlshaber der Alliierten Streitkräfte

ZG 64

A patrol went out to look for a minefield. They got jumped by a platoon of Germans. The sergeant in charge of the patrol said that they beat the Germans off and only lost two men.

"If we go back that way we can get them," he said.

"Who were they?" I asked.

"Nichols. Nichols and Weeks, you know them?"

I knew them.

June 17

We pushed off early. In the distance I could hear the booming of the artillery. Noise is death. Noise is the crackle of a machine gun from somewhere you can't see, or the explosion at the mouth of a German artillery piece four miles away, or a grenade or mortar landing close enough to send some jagged steel through your body. Bobby Joe said that if you hear the sound it means they missed. No, after a while even the noise wounds you.

When it comes from the ships offshore, it sounds different, a deeper sound like an animal exhaling. When it's smaller stuff, it sounds a little bit like a bear cub hissing when it's mad. It's all meant to kill you. That's why everybody is over here: they want to kill me. There are others they want to kill, too, I know, but it's me I'm beginning to feel pity for.

As we get closer to our target, stumbling in the early darkness to someplace named St. Lô, the air gets heavy with the mist and stink of the fighting. The sun catches wisps of smoke rising from the fires where the shells were hitting. It looks almost beautiful.

McCormack said he heard that they were shelling Carentan. "They're hitting it hard," he said.

"I thought they took it already," I answered.

He shrugged. We had heard that they had taken Carentan, but I guess the report was wrong.

June 18

It is an incredibly cold day. My fingers were almost numb this morning. By the time the sun was up, there was fighting all around us. I don't know where the Germans are and I don't know if they know where we are.

We started across a field when a plane strafed us. It didn't get anyone, but it shook us all up. Planes are scary.

We're spread out about two hundred yards, maybe two fifty, depending on the lay of the land. This morning I was closer to the enemy than I have ever been, except for some German prisoners. We went through a little village, St. Andre de l'Epine. A woman was putting her wash out of the windows on the second floor. Lt. Rowe pointed her out to us. It was so normal that we all had to turn and look.

We came up on a half-track that looked out of commission but it opened up on us.

I could hear it. I could hear the bullets hit them. The first two guys in the column went down, one quietly and one screaming. All the guys were firing toward the half-track. I was screaming, and then I saw Bobby Joe running and I went after him. I didn't know what Bobby Joe was going to do. Then I saw him get behind a tree. I was right with him and I saw him pulling the pin on a grenade. I did the same and we threw together as the half-track sent a burst into the tree.

The half-track was spinning around crazily on one track. Two Germans came out of the top. Maybe they were trying to surrender. I don't know. They were hit right away. One fell over the side and the other fell back inside the half-track. Two guys ran over and dropped grenades inside.

I got myself over to the road and saw the first German. He was dead. Then there was more firing and I saw the guys taking cover.

"Scotty! Scotty!"

Bobby Joe was screaming at me. I looked down the road and saw a bunch of Jerries spreading out, taking positions. They were on the road with another half-track. The corporal took a shot at the half-track with a bazooka. He missed, and the half-track's guns turned on him and fired. The corporal jumped into a ditch.

It took three mortar rounds before the half-track was knocked out. The German soldiers kept coming. There were about eighteen or nineteen of them. Then, suddenly, they stopped and started to hightail it.

"Stay down! Stay down!" Lt. Rowe signaled for us to spread out and stay down.

I was on the ground and shooting toward the knot of German soldiers running back toward the trees. About half of them were on the ground, wounded.

We exchanged fire for a while without actually seeing the Germans but knowing they must be there. Then we saw one of them coming forward waving a piece of cloth. They were giving up.

Sgt. Draper, a tough son of a gun, stood up and waved the Germans to come in. They came in, hands raised above their heads, and Sgt. Draper made them sit in a small circle. They weren't too far from me so I went over and took a look at them.

One of them, a bigheaded guy with a gold tooth, was wounded in the side of the face. It looked terrible and he kept wanting to put his hand on it. Sgt. Draper wouldn't let him.

Gearhart, a guy from Martinsburg who speaks German, questioned them. He said that they thought there were only four or five of us, or they wouldn't have come out.

There were seven German soldiers who were healthy enough to keep on walking. The rest were wounded pretty bad or dead. The German corporal told Gearhart that there were thirty guys originally, but the others had either been killed or captured. From where I was, I could see him looking around, wondering what was going to happen to him. Donalds, a heavyset guy with deep set eyes, took the German corporal by the sleeve. He pulled him over to the side of the road where one of our guys lay dead. Lt. Rowe went over to them and stood next to Donalds. I didn't see him saying anything but Donalds just turned and walked away.

Why am I alive? Bullets had flown around me. There were dead Americans lying on the ground. Why am I alive?

One of our wounded guys was calling for his mama. Nobody wanted to hear him or deal with the panic we knew was filling his chest.

"Move out!" Lt. Rowe, who carried a carbine, cradled it in his arms and started down the road.

McCormack got a letter from his folks. He read part of it about how President Roosevelt had told everyone that we were doing a good job and teaching the Germans a lesson.

✳ ✳ ✳

June 19

It's raining. I am miserable. I am cold and sore all over. I picked up a French direction sign. I carried it for about a half-hour before I threw it away. I had been thinking about taking it home, but then it didn't matter anymore. Things that matter in the morning somehow don't matter in the afternoon. By the time the night arrives all that matters is that I am alive. We fought all day yesterday. First we called in artillery and blasted the crap out of the Germans. When we figured it was safe we started toward St. Lô again. I don't know how the Germans lived through the shelling, but they were firing from the rubble. Webster and Kesler got it. I know Kesler's family and feel sorry for them.

All around there are dead animals. They lie in the road and bloat up. I saw a calf lying near a dead cow that was probably its mother.

I know I shot a German today. He was in a window and I shot through the shutter. Maybe I didn't kill him. It's not something I want to think about.

I have to think about it. I was covering the squad as we moved through a circle of buildings. In the middle of the circle was a statue and I was behind it. That's when I looked up and saw the German in the window. I emptied a clip I had just put in. That's eight shots in maybe two or three seconds. The Germans have machine guns. McCormack said they even have machine pistols.

I am afraid of being killed. It's not something I think about all the time, but it's always there. Some guys make jokes about it; some don't even want to mention it.

A tank battalion came by. They stink of grease and oil. Lt. Rowe talked with one of the officers and somehow bummed a radio. We went past the center of the town, past the dead, listening to Glenn Miller.

There are people in these towns, men, women, and children. They are thin, with dark shadows around their eyes. They all look as if they have seen too much, that they can't take any more in. When we pass they stare at us. Sometimes they come out and kiss our hands. I think that somehow they believe that we will end the war for them.

Tomorrow we're going to head back toward St. Andre. It looks like we gain a few hundred yards and then we get pushed back. I wonder if anybody has figured out if we're winning or losing.

Today is my parents' anniversary. I'm glad I didn't die today; it would have messed things up for them.

❋ ❋ ❋

June 20

Don't sit under the apple tree
With anyone else but me
Anyone else but me
Anyone else but me
No! No! No!
Don't sit under the apple tree
With anyone else but me
Till I come marching home

We're camping in an orchard grove. The trees are all shot up, but if I put my head back and look through the branches I can almost be home. I remember when my Boy Scout troop went on a camping trip with a Scout troop from Salem and we spent the night in an apple orchard. It was a glorious feeling to get out in the open and look up at the stars. It's a glorious memory now.

We had a lecture from a chaplain today who wanted to explain why we are over here. Some of the guys started kidding around, saying they had got on the wrong bus — stuff like that. The chaplain (a Catholic, but I didn't mind) started telling us about Hitler and his rise to power. I wrote down some notes.

Hitler — Born in April 1889, became chancellor in 1933, hooked up with Mussolini in 1936, got a bunch of land in the Munich Agreement in 1938, and started the World War in 1939. Then the chaplain gave us the five steps that he said led to us being over here.

"First, people tolerate evil because they see some benefit to themselves," he said. "Then, they feed it in hope that it will turn into something else. Then, they appease it in hope that it will not turn against them. Then, they respect it because they fear it. Finally, someone has to step up and stamp it out! That's the assignment we've been given, to stop this evil that Hitler and his Nazis represent."

I was taking notes, and later Bobby Joe asked me if he could copy the part about the five steps leading to us being in the war.

"One day when I get to explaining all this to my kids, I'm going to need to know what to say," he said.

I wanted to ask the chaplain just how the Nazis had got started and all but he had to get leave and go to the next outfit.

I didn't really know anything about the Nazis before I got into the war. Back when I was a kid I remember Joe Louis beating a German that somebody said was probably a Nazi.

Jerry Villency is alive! Some guys from the Second Battalion came into our outfit, and he was with them. I didn't recognize him at first. He looks so much older. He came over to where I was sitting against the wall of the church grounds and put his hand on my shoulder. Even when he called my name, it took me a while to remember who he was.

"I thought it was you," he said. "It was either you or a pile of rags with a rifle."

"Do I look that bad?"

"You look a lot worse," he said, grinning. He sat down next to me and put his arm around me.

Jerry's about my size and was always a good guy. He had taped his glasses and there was a scab on his forehead.

"You see anybody else we know?" I asked.

"Everybody's dead," he said sadly. "Cliff Lee, Jimmy Wright, so many guys."

"I'm glad you're alive, man," I said.

We hugged each other and I was near to crying just to see him alive. He was sad and tired. We talked for a while, and then some of his guys started moving out and he said he had to go.

"But the Second's not your battalion," I said.

"It is now," he said.

He started away, then stopped and came back. He took off his pack and went through it until he found what he was looking for. Then he gave it to me, waved, and started down the road.

What Jerry had given me was a copy of the *The Roanoke World-News*. It was a paper from right after

D-Day and there was a lot of stuff in it about the landing. None of it made much sense. They had maps showing us landing all over France, from Calais down to the south of France.

What I looked at most was the sports stuff and the advertisements. Jefferson had won a game. I saw names I knew, kids I had left behind who were too young to be in the war. They were still back there, being kids and living well.

There was an article about George Burns and Gracie Allen, who are comedians. When somebody asked them if they were funny when they were home, Gracie said she didn't think so, because she didn't hear anybody laughing.

St. Andre isn't too bad off. There's a really big church right in the center of it. Behind the church there's a cemetery. Some guys went into it and just walked around. There's a few craters where bombs hit, and most of the buildings have some pockmarks from shells.

There's talk about German paratroopers being dropped just past St. Lô. Maj. Howie (I think that's his name, but I don't know why I can't remember it that well) said the Germans are getting set for an all-out counteroffensive. All-out counteroffensive? If they haven't been fighting all-out, what have they been doing? Him saying that really pissed me off. He always gets me mad.

Bobby Joe likes him, though. He says he's really a stand-up kind of guy.

I'm taking a chance on writing to Angie. This is a copy of the letter.

Dear Angie,

In a way you know me and in a way you don't. Being in the war and everything has made me different. What I would like is to have somebody back home to write to, if you don't mind. If you have a steady boyfriend then I will find somebody else, but if you don't I would like to write to you. Even more than that I would like for you to write to me. Sometimes you get so tired and feel so low you need something or someone to bring you back to a point where you are even normal.

Angie, I can't say that I love you but I can say that I have always liked you and hope that you can find it in your heart to like me.

Yours truly,
Scott

The letter isn't strictly true because I am *thatclose* to being in love with Angie Gardiner. If anybody was to ask me how I came to fall in love with her, I would say I don't know, but in my heart I think I just need somebody to be in love with back home.

Two replacement guys joined our unit. Doug Kerlin is from Max Meadows, and J. J. Dandridge is from Winchester. They're scared. They came in on an LST, and when they got to the beach a company of Negro soldiers was loading coffins to take back to the States. That got them scared, but I tried to tell them that it was a good sign.

"Most of the guys that were killed on the first day are buried here," I told them. "We're just mopping up now."

They asked me how many guys were killed during the invasion and I told them that I didn't know, but it was a lot.

They were talking about us sticking together. I don't know if I want any friends over here, but I said okay.

June 21

Everyone was sitting around when a plane came overhead. We all ducked into whatever shelter we could find. The plane — I thought it was a German plane — was in trouble. We watched it stall out, go into a dive, then bank sharply to its left. Soldiers have been trained to stay out of the open; civilians haven't. When the plane came down, I moved a step into the house I was in. The plane first headed for a field and then turned sharply and, because its engines had stopped, silently. It came down like that, catching the sun on its wings, smoke pouring from

55

its fuselage, until it crashed a few feet from a house at the corner of the town square. A small group of civilians tried to get away at the last moment, but it was too late.

June 23

There is fighting every day. You can hear it down the road, or in the distance. Sometimes, when it is cloudy, you can't tell where the sounds of the fighting are coming from. But they are always there. The artillery booms, booms, booms, and then is answered by the echoes in the distant valleys, all sounding like heartbeats coming from the earth. Sometimes, I'd swear that war is a living thing, huge and ugly, that eats up lives.

Squads go out and you don't look at them because you know they might not come back. When the sergeant looks around for volunteers you don't look away, but you don't look at him. Today, me and Billy Joe and Kerlin had to go out and look at a house near the far corner of the village.

"We're moving out tonight and we don't want anybody giving away our position," Lt. Rowe said. "But somebody thought he saw a light in that house and it's not supposed to be occupied. Check it out, and be alert."

Crockett said he was going to go with us.

Checking out a house for enemy soldiers is always hairy. Kerlin said we didn't even have to check it out since we were moving out anyway. Crockett told him if he didn't want to be a soldier he should turn in his M-1 and put on a dress. I was thinking the same thing as Kerlin, and I was glad that I hadn't opened my mouth first.

It was 2010 and still light out as we got near the building. Two kids, about six or seven, were playing on the stairs, and Bobby Joe told them to go away. At first they didn't understand, but then he made a mean face at them and they ran. I watched them run about twenty yards and then the little girl turned and made a face at Bobby Joe.

"I'll go upstairs," Crockett said. "You guys cover me."

"I'll go with you," I said.

"You see anything funny you just hightail it on out of there," Bobby Joe said.

Crockett went stomping up the stairs. If there were any Germans up there, they would have plenty of time to hide. A German with his head down was a lot better than a German with his head up and his sights on us.

There were three stories to the building. Crockett went up the first flight and stopped at the top of the stairs. He looked around and then started to move through the rooms. The floorboards creaked something terrible.

"*Bitte?*"

That was what Crockett was calling out. It means something in German like — hello? or What did you say? We were taught that back in England.

"*Bitte?*"

Crockett pushed into rooms while I covered the halls. Nothing. We checked every room slowly, and I wondered if there was an attic. Some of these old houses don't have regular American attics, but instead something like a half room, almost a crawl space that you could get a cot into if you had to.

There were three rooms on the second floor, and after Crockett had checked all of them, I started up the stairs to the third floor. He stopped me and went past me.

"Get the other guys up here," he said.

I went to the top of the stairs and was about to call Billy Joe when I thought I saw something move in the room at the end of the hall. I turned and saw Crockett, who was almost to the next floor.

My skin went real cold and I could feel my balls shrivel up into a knot. I whistled to let Crockett know I saw something, or thought I did. He whistled back. He didn't know what I meant. At the bottom of the stairs, Bobby Joe looked at me and shrugged.

I wasn't sure. Maybe I hadn't seen anything. Still, I

pointed toward the room. Bobby Joe came up the stairs quickly.

"I'm not sure, but I'll try to flush them out if they're there," I said.

I went up to the next landing where Crockett was.

"It's clear up here," he said.

"I think I might have seen something down below," I said.

I took a grenade and went into the room over the one I thought I had seen a movement in. It was a bedroom, and I pulled the mattress off the bed. I put the mattress on the floor, took two grenades off my belt, and pulled the pins. I held them for a second, then put them on the floor and put the mattress over them. I knew the grenades would bring down the ceiling below us. Me and Crockett moved out of the room.

"Bobby Joe! I'm blowing the ceiling!" I called out a split second before the grenades blew.

A huge puff of smoke came out of the room the grenades were in and Crockett went by me and sprayed some shots toward the walls. From the floor below I heard a series of shots and ran to the stairs.

Bobby Joe was firing into the room and Kerlin had come up and he was firing into the cloud of dust that poured through the doors.

I reached the landing and fired while Bobby Joe re-loaded.

When the smoke cleared we saw two Germans. One was lying on the floor; the other, badly wounded, was on his knees and draped across the seat of the overstuffed couch. The couch had been pushed away from the wall and we moved it out more. There was a hole in the wall where the Germans had been. In the hole there was a radio and a pack of French cigarettes.

"They were shooting at the ceiling," Bobby Joe said.

"They won't be shooting at any more ceilings," Kerlin said.

I thought about Crockett. He hadn't come downstairs. I took the stairs two at a time.

Crockett was stretched out on his back.

"Right through the floor," he said.

"You okay?" I asked.

"I'm going home," he said. "I got to be okay, Jimbo."

Then he groaned. Then he died. That was the way the day ended.

June 24

I am so down over Crockett. I do have to admit that I am thankful it was not me who got killed. A feeling of shame comes over me when I think like that, but that's what's really going through my mind. It's terrible to see guys wounded and killed, but I don't want it to be me that's laying on the side of the road.

Today is Saturday, as if the day of the week had any meaning. The noncoms and officers had a meeting. We could see that something big was going on. After they had their meeting, each company had a meeting. I sat next to Bobby Joe as Col. Dallas talked to us. It was a little gung ho, but all right. He said the Germans are discovering who we are and they don't like it a bit.

"When they were running over the Netherlands and France, they thought we were too weak to fight," he said. "They thought that because we have all kinds of people in our society, whites, blacks, Asians, and Indians, that we didn't have the moral fiber to fight.

"When we entered the war, they thought we wouldn't have the guts of the German soldier. Then they thought they could stop us at the beaches and throw us back into the sea. They had their best at Omaha Beach, and they didn't think that we had the will to make the sacrifices that we have made to carry off the invasion. Now they're desperate. They know who we are, brave and determined men. They know how well we are trained and they know that we're not going to walk away from this fight. They're bringing everything they have to try and hold us here in Normandy. For some reason, they think they can still win this war. Maybe that's the way you think when you consider yourself a master race. I don't know. I do know they will not win because you will not let them win. Soon, very soon, the world will know that, too."

After Col. Dallas finished talking, we got another talk about how we were going to take St. Lô. Well, that was nothing new.

June 25

Went to a badly damaged church. It was beautiful except for the wall behind the altar being blown out. It had a nice effect with the cross silhouetted against the blue sky. Maj. Donovan delivered the sermon and I got to thinking about how things are back home.

"It's five hours earlier here than it is at home," Bobby Joe said after the service. A quartermaster truck had brought up supplies and he was putting on new socks. "Just about now, my mom is making breakfast and my dad is shaving."

"You think they'll pray for us?" I asked.

Soon as I said that, I was sorry I had opened my mouth. Bobby Joe saw me getting sad and threw his old socks at me.

In the afternoon some guys set up a radio and were dancing to Glenn Miller. Some French girls came out to watch them, but they wouldn't dance. J. J. Dandridge came over and told me and Bobby Joe that he had an invite to have dinner with a French family.

"Kerlin's got the crud and can't come," he said.

What Kerlin has is an infection between his toes. After we questioned J. J. about being sure the Frenchies were okay, me, him, and Bobby Joe went to this house. It was a nice place with two women and a girl. One of the women was small, or maybe just thin, and about forty or forty-five years old. She had dark hair and eyes and a sharp, kind of pointy nose. The other one was maybe seventy. She had white hair that she kept touching, pushing it into place. I think she was just nervous. She also had a pointy nose, so I figured that she was the mother of the first woman. The girl was eight years old.

Only the younger woman spoke English and so when we sat down she was the one to say how much she liked Americans. We sat around for a while and then Bobby Joe said he didn't think they had anything to eat.

"They invited me to dinner and said I could bring my friends," J. J. said.

I asked the woman who spoke English if they had any food and she just shrugged.

Bobby Joe told us to wait while he went to get some food. He came back with two five-in-ones. The five-in-ones are what the tankers and truck drivers eat. Each package has five meals in it. We opened one, and the French woman cooked it and we all ate it. We talked a little bit but she didn't speak enough English to make it a real conversation and none of us speak French. We left the other five-in-one with them.

The little girl was younger than Ellen, but she reminded me of my sister. Ellen is older in years, but this little girl was older in a different way. The fighting is taking away the little girl in her and making her old before her time. We soldiers are fighting for our lives. The French, already beaten down by the Germans, are fighting for their souls.

We are on reserve again and it feels good just to rest. We can still hear the sounds of fighting off in the distance, and every once in a while a plane buzzes us and we're diving under something or into a ditch. The scary thing is that the fighting is all around, not just in one direction. Rumor has it that the 101st Airborne is fighting against the Sixth Nazi Parachute Division and a panzer tank outfit. A guy who calls himself a "leftenant" from the English army says they're fighting against tanks east of us.

"The whole line has to hold or we're going to catch it," a sergeant said. "If their tanks break through, then they can swing around and start cutting off individual units."

"Thanks for letting us know the good news," J. J. said. "We were worried the Germans had run out of ideas."

I asked Lt. Rowe if I could see his maps and he let me.

What I saw was that the distance from the beach we landed on to St. Lô is just about the same distance between Roanoke and Bedford. On a good day I can make the trip to Bedford in thirty minutes. We have been fighting like crazy and we haven't taken twenty five miles yet.

June 26

Some units from the 115th are moving toward St. Lô. They look ready for a good fight. I have to admit they look sharper than we do.

I am getting used to being relaxed. Bobby Joe said that he thinks the Germans are retreating. I said that I agreed with him, but I don't really. I am hoping they are retreating more than thinking it.

Got a letter! Yes!

Mom said that everything is fine at home. Danny got a job at Furbursh's drugstore for the summer and Ellen got a two-week pass to the movies for collecting the most newspapers for the war effort. She said everybody is proud of us and praying for us. She wants me to write if I have a chance, but not to worry about it if I am too busy.

That probably means that she hasn't received my letters. I spoke to Lt. Hanken, and he said that as far as he knows, the mail is getting through. He is worried that his letters aren't getting through, too.

June 27

A guy stepped on a mine today just twenty feet behind the mess truck, so they made us look for more mines. The Germans have their minefields marked, but naturally they take up the signs when they go. There are three kinds of mines over here. The biggest is the tank mine which is not that bad because it won't go off if just a person steps on it. The small ones, the anti-personnel mines, are scary.

"I'd rather be looking for tank mines," J. J. said.

I don't think J. J. is all that bright. *Anybody* would rather look for a tank mine. All you have to do is stick your bayonet in the ground and you can find them. Then you need to dig under them carefully to make sure the Germans haven't booby-trapped them by putting an anti-personnel mine under the tank mine. The anti-personnel mines go off too easy. The Germans have one mine that will go off as soon as you step on it. It'll either blow off part of your leg or kill you outright. Another one they have doesn't go off right away — it shoots up in the air when you take your foot off it. Then it blows up so it gets you in your body. They call them Bouncing Bettys.

I was probing around for a half-hour when I hit something I thought was a mine. What I wanted to do was to shoot it, but I had to dig it out. It turned out to be a rock. Still scared me to death.

June 28

Three new guys showed up. Their fatigues are nice and shiny. They said they were over from Fort Dix and had been with the First Army. We got into an argument about whether the King Sisters or the Andrews Sisters sing the best. The new guys were saying that we didn't know what we were talking about when me and Bobby Joe said the King Sisters sing the best. Everybody got mad at them. They haven't been around long enough to make a lot of noise about anything.

Kerlin is going back to England. We heard him being chewed out and then saw him packing up his gear.

"What happened?" J. J. asked him.

"My crud got worse," he said.

He took off his shoes and we looked at his feet. The infections between his toes had gotten worse. It looked pretty bad. The skin between the toes was cracked and he couldn't walk without limping.

"When I get rid of the crud I'll be back," he said.

When he left on a truck with two other guys who had been wounded, I think we all had mixed feelings. One thing for sure, he isn't going to be in the fighting for a while.

Naturally we had an inspection of all our feet and socks. Everybody who had dirty socks on or sores on their feet got chewed out, same as back in the States.

June 29

A stream of guys from the 115th, the same that passed through a few days ago, came back from fighting at St. Lô.

"We got chewed up and spit out!" a guy with his head bandaged said. "They were dug in and waiting for us. They got 88s, mortars, panzers, everything. One of their panzers knocked out two of our tanks like they were toys."

Bobby Joe asked how many guys they had lost, and this guy said he didn't know. He was in a ten-man squad, with two machine guns instead of one, and five guys were killed and him and another guy wounded.

"They waited until we were in the town, then they attacked our flank with panzers that were in the buildings," the guy said. He took a lit cigarette somebody offered him. "They attacked the right flank and then started firing down on us from the buildings. We were shooting back, but we couldn't see what we were shooting at. Finally, we spotted some infantry guys coming toward us. They looked like paratroopers, maybe a company of them, trying to cut us off. I don't think anybody would have made it if our machine gunner hadn't stayed back to cover us."

"He get out?"

"No."

St. Lô is a railroad town and a communications center for the Germans. The longer they hold it, the better the chance they can get enough reinforcements to start pushing us back toward the beaches. Some of the guys from the 115th said the Germans have placed their guns to cover all the main streets so you can't get more than a squad involved in a firefight on a particular street.

"You can't send a whole company down a narrow city street," a sergeant said. "You have to fight them doorway to doorway, building by building."

The guys from the 115th looked beat-up. It didn't make us feel good to see them like that.

A captain just told us to get our gear together. We're moving out.

June 30

We moved toward St. Lô last night. Halfway there we got hit by artillery. Two trucks got knocked out in the first barrage and at first everybody thought it was mortars, but it wasn't. We moved forward to change the range of the artillery in case they had a spotter who saw us on the road. That looked like it worked because they were walking their artillery back the other way. But then we got hit by a new barrage and got into a firefight with what looked like a battalion. We pulled back fast, and for a while it took all the nerve we had not to panic. The Germans are good at what they do.

For some reason I was thinking that we should win all the fights because we're the good guys. It doesn't work that way. I don't want to question God or anything, but this fighting against the Germans doesn't work the way I thought it would.

The days off did me a little good but now that we're back into it I think I have to get used to the fighting again. No, I won't get used to it. I just hope I live through it.

When we got out of range, we picked up some more tank support. Some of the officers are saying that their tanks are better than ours. When we get into big tank fights our tanks get knocked out quick. But our infantry guys need tank support of some kind when we go up against the panzers. You don't shoot an M-1 at a German panzer and live to tell about it.

Found out that Col. Metcalf was wounded. Hope he'll be okay. Dallas is taking his place.

I'm sorry I wrote to Angie. Maybe she's going to think I'm stupid because I don't really know her. Maybe she won't get the letter.

July 1

Lt. Hanken was making a list of the wounded and dead and Paul Huntington's name was on it. I think he did some yardwork for Angie's family once. Also, Kerlin's name was listed on it as being dead, but I told Hanken that he only came down with the crud.

Bobby Joe has a terrible bruise on one side of his face.

"I was behind a tank when it got hit," he said. "When the shell hit the tank it knocked it back three feet. I was just lucky it didn't roll over me."

If I once thought I would make it home safe, that thought is gone now. They keep replacing guys, and sooner or later they're going to have to replace me. No use worrying about it.

Also, found out that Kerlin *is* dead. The truck they were taking him back on got wiped out. I'm glad I didn't know him better.

July 3

More replacements arrived. They seem like nice guys. They're coming in already scared. I wonder what they're being told. We're being allowed to sleep late, but then we do training maneuvers, weapon drills, and target practice. Bobby Joe thinks that they want the new men to get used to the noise. Lt. Rowe says that we have to get accustomed to working with each other.

"What we do depends largely on how we make out as a team," he said. "If we work together we'll be all right."

This is not my idea of work. What he really means is if we fight together we'll be all right.

Off in the distance the constant *boom-boom-boom* of artillery never stops. I think that if I make it back home I will always hear it. I'm tired today. I can't sleep soundly over here. Sometimes I dream, but most of what I dream about is fighting. In every dream I find a dead guy who just looks up at me. Sometimes I think I recognize the dead guy. Mikey . . . Wojo . . . Crockett . . . Kerlin. I'm forgetting some of the names already. Back home I never dreamed.

The officers are getting closer to the men. They're not friendlier or anything like that. They just know that we all know the same thing that they know about the last few weeks. The officers went over the plans to take St. Lô and tried to show us just what we have to do. All the towns in France are in valleys, and there are hills that overlook them. What we are going to do is to take the hills around St. Lô. On the maps, the hills are named according to how high they are. The higher the hill, the tougher it's going to be to take it. The Germans dig in and shoot down on you and it's just terrible. There aren't any easy battles, just fights that I somehow make it through.

We found a shallow grave in the back of a building. The way we found it was the rain had washed away some of the dirt and there were boots sticking up from the ground. The company commander had some of the new guys dig up enough to figure out that the bodies were Germans. Then we covered them back up.

July 4

Woke up feeling pretty gung ho because of the Fourth of July. We passed a French house and a young boy waved at us and called out, "Hey, Yanks!" That made me feel good.

I wonder if there were any parades going on back home. I know there must have been plenty. Picnics, too. Heard on the radio that the Russians took Minsk. It must be really good to take back your own city.

July 5

Went on a patrol last night to capture a German. Me, Lt. Rowe, and two sergeants jumped off at 2300.

"We want to get one guy and bring him back alive to headquarters," Lt. Rowe said. "The best way to do this is to find one or two guys off by themselves and snatch them. If we see a target, we'll split into two-man teams. Collins, you stick with me. The team that gets the prisoner will secure him and move out. The other team will cover."

We taped our dog tags to our chests so they wouldn't

make noise and put leaves and twigs in the webbing over our helmets to break up the outline. I put black grease on my cheekbones and chin.

There were Germans moving in the vicinity of Cerisy Forest and we headed there. One of the sergeants said that he knew there was American infantry in the northern part of the woods.

"That's why the Germans send patrols," he said.

So we were going to look for a German patrol that might be looking for American prisoners. I was carrying six grenades along with my rifle and a small carbine bayonet I had picked up from supply. I had my regular M-1 bayonet on my cartridge belt as well.

The night was warm, even though it was raining lightly as we moved along the hedgerows toward the road that led to Cerisy. There was a moon, and every so often it found a hole in the clouds and lit up the fields. At 2400 we saw a light coming from what looked like a small hut. We got down on the ground and started crawling along a ridge toward the light, with the two sergeants about 25 yards to our right. When Lt. Rowe and I got within ten yards of where the light was, it went out. I froze, thinking they must have spotted us.

We heard a noise and saw the outline of a figure coming toward us. He had something in his hands and I thought it was a machine gun. I pushed the safety of my rifle. It was already off. A cold trickle of sweat ran under my chin strap and down my neck.

The figure stopped just as the moonlight broke through the trees. It was just light enough to see a German soldier standing about fifteen feet away from me. I glanced over at where I thought Lt. Rowe was and couldn't see him. I looked back at the German and saw that he was fumbling with his belt. My mind said "grenade," and I aimed my rifle the best I could. Then I saw him dropping his pants.

When he squatted down I saw Lt. Rowe lift his hand and signal me.

Fifteen feet is one hash mark on a football field. I made it in a hot second. I grabbed the German around the neck and pulled him backward. Lt. Rowe got over him and put both his hands over the guy's face. I thought for a while he was going to kill him but then he let him go.

The German was gasping when Lt. Rowe released his face. Then Lt. Rowe put his hands over his face again. It was like choking down a wild horse.

I could feel the German's heart throbbing in his throat. His eyes were wild, and he was trying to bring his hands together, trying to pray.

Lt. Rowe pulled a hood from his shirt and put it over the guy's face.

"Heinreich?" A voice came from the hut. Another German. "Heinreich?"

Lt. Rowe had his hands over the face of the German we had down and I had the small bayonet pressed into his neck.

The German calling to him listened for a while, shrugged, and went back into the hut.

We dragged away the German we had captured and met up with the two sergeants. The German still had the hood over his face and I think he was kind of whimpering.

When I got back to camp Lt. Rowe said I had done a good job. Two officers took the hood off the German, searched him, then put him against a wall and started questioning him. His hands were shaking and he was stuttering. He tried to wipe the snot off his face, but the American officers wouldn't let him lift his hands. I couldn't understand anything being said, so I went to look for my squad and bunked down for the rest of the night.

July 6

Woke up early this morning and felt strange. Don't know why, but I did. Got some coffee. Mom is going to be surprised to find out I drink coffee, because I never did like it back home. I was thinking about Danny and Ellen and Dad and drinking the coffee when I saw some planes in the distance. They weren't more than a few miles away.

The sun hadn't burned off the haze yet so you couldn't see anything too clearly, but you could hear the angry buzz of the plane engines. They were strafing some ground position, going high in the sky, and then swooping down through the early-morning mist. From where I sat at the base of a tree, I could see the dark puffs of smoke, like black flowers, fill the sky around the planes.

"Would you rather be up there or down here?" J. J. asked me.

I hadn't seen him coming and jumped a little.

"It doesn't make a difference to me," I said. "Long as I don't miss the party."

Lt. Hanken asked me to take the casualty list to battalion headquarters. I said okay (as if I had a choice) and asked him if I could requisition some extra socks.

"Can't hurt trying," he said with a big grin.

I like Lt. Hanken and the thought came to me that I hope he doesn't get killed.

The jeep we took into battalion headquarters stayed in the tracks of another truck that had gone along the same path.

"That way," the driver said, "I know I won't hit any mines."

When I got to battalion I turned in the casualty list and the major said that he was relieved to see that we didn't take many casualties. We only had two wounded in action and one guy, somebody named Maddox, listed as killed in action.

"We weren't in any battles," I said. "He was just out on patrol."

I didn't get any extra socks.

On the way back I wondered about Maddox, and if somebody would be saying that it was a light day if I was the only one killed from my company. I told myself to think positive thoughts.

The officers got a movie, but they couldn't get the projector to work. The tech sergeant who was supposed to show it got upset, but nobody really cared. After two hours they finally got the thing working and started the movie right in the middle. It didn't matter. There were pretty girls and some guys speaking American. That's all I needed.

Maj. Howie came to the movie. Most of the guys who know him like him. They say he makes things simple. Something is either the right thing to do or it's not the right thing.

Some guys found some French wine and some soap. I got two (count 'em) bars of the soap and gave one to Bobby Joe.

"If I can't find nobody cuter than you, will you marry me?" he said when I gave him the soap.

He doesn't know it, but I am trying to get the can of Spam his mother sent him. I have given him a roll of toilet paper and the soap. After a while I think he will feel guilty and give me the Spam. Anyway, I hope so.

July 8

All week long we have been training, even marching some. I feel stupid marching. I hope the Germans don't see us. There were some tracks that looked as if a German patrol had come through our perimeter. That freaked everybody out. Not only that, but we got an order over the radio to move 500 yards down to the road. Guys were packing up to move out when we got the word that the order was false. They've got Germans who speak perfect English giving fake orders. Scary.

Bobby Joe brought over a cartoon that he got from *Stars and Stripes* or *Yank*. He thought it was the funniest cartoon in the world. It showed two GIs in England, and one was saying that if anybody volunteered to go to France to get away from the buzz bombs, they were a coward.

That wasn't funny to me but I laughed anyway so Bobby Joe wouldn't feel bad.

July 9

Another rumor. The war is just about over! The Germans are just waiting for a good time to surrender. I believe this is the real deal. I'm sure about it. We're still on thirty-minute alert, which means that we have to be ready to fight with thirty minutes of notice. Bobby Joe said he doesn't need thirty minutes.

"I sleep with my rifle, I eat with my rifle, I go to the bathroom with my rifle," he said. "You know how they say some dogs look like their owners?"

"Yeah?"

"Well, my M-1 is getting to look like me," he said.

We're bivouacking in the woods. We still have patrols and I was stuck on one with a squad of replacements. We were about thirty minutes out, going along the edge of a clearing, when we spotted a German patrol. There were about fifteen of them and eight of us. I got everybody down and we opened fire on the Germans. On my second clip my M-1 jammed. I had to roll over on my back, open the bolt, and clear the breech by hand. It was my first jam.

When I got back from the patrol I took my rifle apart, piece by piece, and cleaned it. Bow-koo (that's "a lot" in French) scary.

July 10

Two signal corps guys got it today. One was in a tree stringing wire. He got hit and his gaffs, the hooks they used to climb trees, were still dug in and his belt was still on so he didn't fall. Terrible.

July 10, evening!

Got two letters from Mom and newspapers from Roanoke. Mom got my letters. She said everything was blacked out but that she thanked God that I'm alive. I'm so glad she knows I'm alive. I'm so excited over the letters I don't know what to do. Mom said they had services at Second Presbyterian and the Jefferson High School band played. Afterward my name was mentioned with all the guys serving in the armed forces. She said that the Russians were beating the Nazis back in the east and that she thought the war was soon going to be over. Yes! She sent me a picture of the whole family that made me cry just to see it. It is a studio picture, with her and Dad sitting on a kind of couch and Danny and Ellen standing up behind them. I can't believe how big Danny looks. Wow! I hope the war is over before he gets into it.

There was another picture, wrapped up in tissue paper, and I put it aside for later.

Mom went on to say that Ellen's school, Morningside, collected a bunch of fat for the war effort. They didn't collect as much as West End, but it was still a lot and I am proud of her.

J. J. came over with two guys from Christianburg and when they found out I had newspapers from home they asked me to read them out loud. They didn't want to read the news themselves. What they wanted was for all of us to sit around and hear what was going on back home. I read the papers and I couldn't help but get emotional. The papers are *The Roanoke World-News* from June 10th and June 12th and I read just about everything I could in them out loud.

They have a map of France and we found Saint-Lô on it. It is just a dot but at least they know where we are going to be fighting. There was a mention that in Italy the preachers were complaining that the Italian girls are fooling around with American soldiers and that got everybody excited. The St. Louis Cardinals are in first place in the National League and the St. Louis Browns are in first place in the American League. I had eaten in Norman's Restaurant in Salem a lot of times and we saw they are looking for people to work there. J. J. said that he was going to leave right away and go apply for a job.

When I got to the part where they were advertising for a colored man to work in a garage, Bobby Joe said he would apply for that job because he feels kind of colored. I guess he just wants to get back home and I don't blame him.

Then we got to a part where they were talking about us! They didn't say anything about the 116th or the 29th because of its being a secret, but they said that Americans were striking through the Cerisy Forest, headed toward St. Lô along the main road and cutting off the German supply lines. It said the Germans are packing troops and armor into St. Lô, which they want to hold at all costs.

We checked out some other jobs. Sears is hiring and there are jobs for experienced mechanics at $40 a week. One of the guys from Christianburg said that if he made $40 a week he would buy a Cadillac car and a portable Emerson radio and drive around Roanoke all day with a blonde on his arm.

The last thing I read was about the movies. Nothing good was playing except a western with "Wild Bill" Elliott and Gabby Hayes. They got into an argument about who is best, "Wild Bill" Elliott or Gene Autry. I didn't say anything because they are all fellow soldiers and everything, but I never considered Gene Autry to be half the cowboy that "Wild Bill" Elliott is.

I put the picture of the family in my pocket. Then I took out the other picture. It was Angie. Angie has blue-gray eyes and dark blonde hair and she wears glasses but in the picture she sent she isn't wearing her glasses. She has on this little smile and her head is turned to one side like she is glad to be looking out of the picture at me. I started to put the picture back in the tissue when I saw there was something written on the back of it. I turned it over and it said, *Dear Scotty, would it sound too stupid if I said "I love you"? Angie.*

No, it wouldn't sound too stupid.

July 11

I have been awake since 0100 when I was awakened by incoming artillery. We were scrambling in the darkness as the Jerries pounded us with their artillery. It just kept coming and coming and coming. I got under a truck with Lt. Hanken, and he was praying the whole time.

Sometimes you can take a lot and sometimes it just gets to you. A light rain was falling, not enough to put out the fires from the shells, but enough to make the air so heavy the stink from the incoming didn't drift off. It was so thick some guys thought we were being gassed. Most of us have lost our gas masks, so it didn't matter. There wasn't anything we could do about it.

The shelling went on until almost three o'clock. It got to me good. My body was shaking with it. Soon as it stopped, we got orders to move out. I crawled out from under the truck and found a place to pee.

"Jerry's got to be coming in behind that barrage," Bobby Joe said.

"Could be." That's all I could say. My mouth was dry and I was spooked clear through.

As we formed up I could see a detail gathering up the wounded and tagging the dead. They were using flashlights because the main generators were out. A medic was going through treating minor wounds.

"Where you hit?" he asked me.

"You okay?" Bobby Joe looked at me.

I looked at where Bobby Joe was looking and saw that I had blood on my side. I wasn't hit. I ran back to where I had been under the truck and got down on my hands and knees. Lt. Hanken was lying there. He wasn't dead. He was kind of whimpering. The medic had come with me and he shined his light on Hanken. You could tell he was hurt bad. His face was drained white and his teeth were chattering.

We helped pull him out and got some blankets to put over him.

"Let's go! Let's go!" The orders came and me and Bobby Joe each gave Lt. Hanken a pat before we got back to our squad.

We formed skirmish lines and started along the ridge line toward St. Lô. I remembered what the newspaper had said about the Germans wanting to hold it at all costs.

We moved up and took positions on the ridge and dug in. Our artillery opened up at 0600. They were shooting over our heads, but they were doing it with a vengeance. I figured we would be moving out any minute to go in behind the artillery or the Germans would be coming after us. Lt. Rowe was in a foxhole near us and he told a sergeant that our tanks were moving out away from us.

"Where're they going?" the sergeant asked.

"Couvains."

It's the same towns over and over again. I wonder if the Germans are feeling as discouraged as I am.

The road and fields are littered with dead animals. The decaying flesh smells awful. We buried dead soldiers, even German soldiers, but no one buried the animals. The smell is something you can't get used to no matter what you tell yourself.

No sooner had we dug our foxholes than we received the order to move out. No sooner had we got out of our foxholes than we got attacked from our left flank. I think the guys that attacked us were as surprised to see us there as we were to see them. They hit us with mortars and machine-gun fire. We had them outnumbered, and they started retreating down into a gulley. When one of our squads got too close to them, they opened up with a flamethrower and our guys backed off long enough for them to get away.

If I die I don't want it to be with a flamethrower.

A squad went out and searched the bodies of the dead Germans. They took their papers, ID and stuff, and sent it in a dispatch to battalion.

At 1400 we moved into position along a front with the rest of the regiment.

July 13

Me and Bobby Joe are dug in good. I started the hole and Bobby Joe finished it. He was digging in real deep. The shelf we stand on is the right height but the grenade sump, where we hope a grenade will go in case one lands in our hole, is too deep, and I told him so.

"I'm going AWOL," he said. "Digging right to China."

July 13, evening

Nothing to eat but crackers and jelly.

When the First and Third Battalions dug in the Second was still moving forward. Capt. King took a patrol and went out to look for them. He came back and said that they were chewed up pretty bad. There's a German outfit, bigger than a battalion, between them and us, and another German outfit, maybe paratroopers, on their flank.

I'm thinking about Jerry Villency, but I don't want to. I hope God is taking care of him. I heard that Capt. Heffner made a deal with the Germans to let them get their wounded and get some of ours back. It's strange making deals like that.

"We're trying to hang on to being civilized," Lt. Rowe said.

July 14

Happy birthday, Mom! I hope you get to read this and know I was thinking of you on your birthday. It's pouring rain. Even the artillery is quiet. Two patrols went out with ammo and medical supplies to take to the Second Battalion. Lt. White led one patrol and Lt. Williams led the other one. The Germans have reinforced their position between us and the Second Battalion and things don't look good for our guys.

July 17

We control the ridge and the Germans want to take it back from us. Lt. Rowe came back from the battalion meeting and said that we were going to move out early to take Martinville.

"The objective is to take the road and hold it," Lt. Rowe said. "That's a clear shot into St. Lô."

"They got tanks up there?" J. J. asked.

Lt. Rowe didn't answer.

We moved out at 0430. It was still dark and most of us were hungry. I had eaten everything I carried and got some canned peaches from Bobby Joe, who had scrounged them from a medic. Maj. Howie had given the order to keep as quiet as possible. Rumor had it that the commander of the 29th had given the order for us to take Martinville and that it looked risky. Eventually we were supposed to hook up with the Second Battalion, which was still cut off.

We were on the high ground and moved in without artillery. Our first sighting of the Germans was when we saw their fires. They were making breakfast! We opened up and they came back with mortars and fire from tanks. From the ridge, we could see them through the smoke. The muzzle fire from their rifles twinkled from the hedgerows like thousands of angry fireflies. Their heavy weapons were firing to the top of the ridge and over it. We had caught them off guard, but they were fighting back hard. They did have some armor, but it was on the wrong side of the hedgerows, and when they tried to get them over, two were knocked out with bazooka fire.

They kept up the shelling at the top of the ridge. They were still shooting high, but it kept our heads down. We could recognize guys from their paratrooper units and we saw a batch of them. Some of them were carrying flamethrowers, and we tried to pin them down.

"Here they come!"

They came in a line just as the sun came up over the

fields south of the road. They were pouring across the road and concentrating their fire to our left on A Company. They were trying to get a front attack and a flank attack.

Maj. Howie was moving down the line with his radio man. Lt. Rowe got a corporal on the radio to find out if they wanted us to retreat up the ridge. But we could see the guys down the road from us and we knew what they were doing. Lt. Rowe got on the radio, listened for a minute, then nodded.

"Fix bayonets!" he called out.

That said it all. We weren't going anywhere. Maj. Howie was going to have us hold the ridge if we had to fight the Germans hand to hand. I got out my bayonet and put it on the end of my rifle. In the early-morning sunlight, I saw Bobby Joe's profile. His lips were tight, pulled back. I couldn't see his eyes under his helmet.

The Germans started up the ridge and we began throwing grenades at them. Their first wave slowed as they hit the bushes and the grenades tore into them. They made a short run up the ridge but started falling back as more grenades came down on them. We were throwing everything we had and they were coming with everything they had. One of their flamethrowers got hit, and some of their own guys got it. They started retreating across the road, and our mortar guys gave them more to worry about.

We started digging in, but before we had our holes dug, they came at us again. The guys who had taken their bayonets off their rifles put them back on again.

This time their rush was even stronger, fanatical. But they were coming uphill, and we were shooting down at them and throwing whatever grenades we had left. We beat them back again, and this time we could see them moving out across the fields. We had held.

Maj. Howie came down the line, stopping and telling everybody how good they had done.

"If we had gone over the ridge they would have been shooting down at us," Lt. Rowe said afterward. "We might have been cut off, too."

The way things worked out was that since the Germans were retreating, we were able to hook up with the Second Battalion. Trucks from headquarters company came up and started taking out the dead and wounded.

They needed a lot of trucks.

July 19

We are in reserve, which means we're not fighting for the moment but are on thirty-minute alert again. Maj. Howie was killed. I never got to talk to him and I didn't really know that much about him except for the fact that he was one of those guys who made things simple. He figured out what was the right thing to do and then he did it. At first my not knowing him didn't stop me from thinking bad things about him. The truth was that he was the kind of brave soldier and brave man that I don't think I can ever be, and that bothers me. I wonder if his soul was just bigger than mine or if somehow I am incomplete.

We took St. Lô yesterday. I watched as guys from the 115th moved down the Martinville road into the city. It was a road I helped take. Bobby Joe and J. J. went into the city to get some food from the 115th. Bobby Joe brought back some K rations and some real eggs. We cooked them in his pot and they tasted almost as good as my mom's eggs. I asked J. J. what St. Lô looked like and he said he didn't know.

"It's nothing but a big pile of rubble," Bobby Joe said. "Ain't nothing standing in that town. Every building is shot or bombed down, every street is filled with stones from what used to be buildings or broken-down vehicles.

"They took Maj. Howie's body into the town," Bobby Joe said. "It's right in the main square on a pile of stones and covered by a flag."

July 23

North of St. Lô. We moved out of the area in style, riding on tanks and antitank tracked vehicles. Got to ride in a tank. No way I would want to be cooped up in one of those things for long.

We rode through the city, although we didn't have to, so the guys could see what they had been fighting for. The convoy stopped and we looked around for maybe fifteen minutes. The whole town is in ruins. A Frenchman, he was an old guy with dark shiny eyes that made his face look younger than his stooped body, took Bobby Joe by the hand. Bobby Joe towered over the guy, but he went with him as he took him halfway down the street and pointed out what had once been a church.

"Notre Dame," he said.

Bobby Joe started telling the old guy that we had a college called Notre Dame in our country. From where I stood I could see that the old man wasn't listening. He kept repeating "Notre Dame" over and over as tears ran down his wrinkled face. I walked back to the troop carrier I had been riding on.

Two letters from home. One from Mom and the other one from Ellen. Mom read some stuff by some guy named Walter Cronkite and wants to know if I saw him over here. She said she just found out Mrs. Lucado's son is missing in action. I don't know who that is. She said she hasn't been getting mail from me but thinks in her heart that I'm all right.

The letter from Ellen is about how she was playing

softball in the park and got two home runs. She wants to know if there are colored soldiers fighting over here.

No letter from Angie, which got me down a little. But since we're in reserve again I can't get too down. I was lying down the other night when I started thinking about St. Lô. I feel bad about the piles of stones that all those lives paid for. Then I think about Roanoke, and I know what the old man was crying about.

July 24

The story going around is that Hitler's own guys tried to kill him last Thursday! He's wounded and might have to give up command of the Nazi army! This thing has got to be over soon. I bet they know back home if any of this is real or just another stupid rumor. I hope it's real. Hitler is a creep and doesn't deserve to live.

We're on thirty-minute alert. All day long our planes are overhead flying toward wherever the Germans think they can hide.

I don't know if I can get rested even though that's what we're supposed to be doing here. You can't really rest when you're on thirty-minute alert and might have to move out any minute. Wrote another letter to Mom to let her know I'm all right. Couldn't think of a lot to say, though.

Dear Mom,

We're in a rest area. The churches in this town are really old and you can tell that before the war they were really something. The French people are worse off, a lot worse off, than we are. I was speaking to a French woman and she told me her entire family was killed by shelling. I hope it was German artillery and not ours. But at St. Lô I know that the French were caught between us and the Nazis and a lot of them died.

The French try to live normal lives, which is strange in a way and in another way it's all they can do. This morning they were clearing away some rubble and found three bodies under a pile of wooden beams. Awful.

Tell Ellen that there are some colored soldiers over here. Most of them are driving trucks, or with the engineers or grave registration. Back at the beach, the guys who brought in the barrage balloons were colored.

Your loving son,
Scott

I told Bobby Joe about the colored guys bringing in the barrage balloons and he said that when he becomes president he's going to let all the colored guys fight right up front.

"Just to show them I'm a good guy," he said.

July 26

Okay, I can't believe this. Col. Dwyer comes around and starts talking to Lt. Rowe and some other officers. Then they call me and a guy from headquarters company over and Col. Dwyer says we're both going to be sergeants!

"We need some men leading this thing that have experience," he said. "You men are old-timers."

When Col. Dwyer left, Lt. Rowe told me I looked pretty stupid standing there with my mouth open.

"If I didn't think you could handle the job I wouldn't have recommended you for it," he said.

"I never made corporal," I said.

"If we run into any more engagements like we did at St. Lô," he said, "you're liable to make lieutenant before you make corporal."

When I told Bobby Joe he said that they must be scraping the bottom of the barrel, but then he said he would rather follow me than some guy fresh off the boat. That made me feel good. Also, I made a mental note to call a fight an "engagement" the way Lt. Rowe had.

July 27

We're still on thirty-minute alert. I haven't fired my rifle in an entire week. Cleaned it three times and also sharpened my bayonet, which I hope I will never have to use.

Two guys were hit by sniper fire. One died. Our guys killed the sniper. He was a kid. A Nazi kid.

I think the war is just about over. We'll probably stay here for another week or so and then start withdrawing and going home. The Germans have had it.

July 28

At 0530 we were up, and were on the move by 0800. Moved generally south to St. Samson. Lots of grumbling because the rumor was that we were headed home. Then there was some grumbling that we had to do all the dirty work because we were experienced or, as Col. Dwyer put it, old-timers.

I saw guys getting careless. A couple of guys got hit because they weren't alert. We also ran into a bunch of 115th guys and some Brits. I like the Brits. Back in England, the regular English people seemed a little soft and schoolmarmish, but the guys over here doing the fighting are a bunch of rough-and-ready guys. Our guys are getting down because they're so tired. The officers are running drills to keep us sharp. I guess being mad at them is better than relaxing too much.

"The next time America has a war we should have one with Delaware," J. J. said.

"Delaware is American!" Bobby Joe said.

"Well, won't they be surprised when we attack them?" J. J. said.

July 31

Fourteen days before my eighteenth birthday. I'm never going to make it. We attacked Moyon. It looked like a regular firefight at first, then we got hit on the flank by a panzer unit. Lord, there is nothing scarier than a German tank. The tanks stirred up a lot of dust as they came at us. Their infantry followed the tanks, and we were beat back. There was one block where four of our guys fell in the middle of the street. I could see the tanks coming toward them as we moved out.

"Bazooka! Bazooka!"

Lt. Rowe was calling for a bazooka, anything that would stop the tanks from running over those men. But it was too late. We fired at them with our rifles, but it wasn't any use.

The panzers didn't want to come away from the buildings, where our antitank guns could get a clear shot at them. We got away, but not before losing a lot of men. We attacked again and called in artillery.

It took four tries and a lot of wounded and killed

before we got the Germans to retreat from Moyon. Then we moved in and they shelled us all night long as usual.

Lt. Rowe broke a tooth from grinding his teeth together. Talk about tense!

August 1

Everything is messed up. We've been fighting on the outskirts of Moyon for days. We push the Germans out and then they push us out. It's another town that's going to be blown to bits.

The radio talks about buzz bombs in London and in the surrounding countryside. They say that there's no warning. All of a sudden they're just there — *Ka-boom!* The radio announcer said that the bombs are "not an effective way of fighting a war." Tell that to the people who are killed.

The units are mixed up again. It's like the days following the landing where you had to go around looking for your unit. The officers can't give orders because they can't find their men.

August 4

Where are they getting their artillery from? Wherever we are they seem to have us zeroed in. The pounding keeps coming and coming. It rolls around and grumbles as you are crouched against some tree or some rock or some truck, hoping that you're safe. But you are never safe. The Jerries are shooting from three to five miles away. They can't see you. They just send out their shells and hope that the shells will somehow find you. They are finding so many men.

The number of dead animals, stiff and bloated in the streets and along the paths to the city, is as many as it was at St. Lô. The stink is the same, too.

I can tell the difference between the smell of a dead cow and a dead man. The things you learn in war.

August 5

Meeting. My first as sergeant. Lt. Rowe and the other junior officers and noncoms, including me, were given our objectives for an attack on Vire. We're leapfrogging like crazy. One unit attacks, establishes a foothold, and the next unit goes through them and attacks the next objective.

I found Vire on the map. The coordinates are 632317.

"As per usual the town is in a valley and it's surrounded by hills," Col. Dwyer said. "And as usual we're going to fight our way up those hills and take them from the Jerries. From what we've been told, they're digging in to stay and they intend to fight to the last man. Since the attempt on Hitler's life, all their officers are trying to prove they're loyal. Keep that in mind. Good luck."

The latest rumor, which means that we got it within the last twenty-four hours, is that the attack on Hitler never happened. Col. Dwyer wouldn't have said that if it hadn't. But every time I hear about the Nazis it's something about them digging in and fighting hard, which means there are more tough days ahead.

"We're responsible for this small section, right here." Lt. Rowe pointed to a spot on the line drawing he had made of Hill 203, our battalion's objective. "We're going to send two squads and try to secure this little path right here. According to the Resistance in this area, the path leads all the way up the hill.

"Once we take this path we secure it and hold it while the next two squads move up and secure the next level area. Then we move up while Charlie Company secures the base. At that point we're going to be relieved by the Ninth Infantry. We move out at 2300. Any questions?"

I thought about making a smart remark about that being past my bedtime, but decided against it. When I got back to our platoon, Bobby Joe and J. J. were waiting for me. They wanted to know what we were going to be doing. If I ever get to be an officer I will always tell my men what they will be doing and what dangers they will face.

"How does it look?" Bobby Joe asked.

"We can get it done," I said.

August 7

I'm out of food and toilet paper. I must have left my rations somewhere. Don't know where. Our battalion took the lead. We found a stream and started up it. The water flowed against us as we went along at a quick pace. A light rain started at 1500 and I reversed my rifle, turning it butt up as I walked. We weren't getting any incoming artillery, and I figured either the Jerries didn't know where we were or didn't care.

They had to know we were coming. The same way they knew we were coming when the invasion started. I wondered what they thought of us. A couple of guys who speak German read us the surrender leaflets the Ninth Air Force planes had dropped on the Jerries. The leaflets said that they thought we couldn't beat them, but we were beating them, and that everything they had been told about how invincible they were wasn't true.

But they were still in the hills and in the cities of France and leaving a trail of bodies behind. A lot more were giving up than when we first landed, but a lot were still fighting hard.

Lt. Col. Cassell was leading the march in the stream.

"What are you going to do when this is all over?" Lt. Rowe asked me. I knew he meant the war.

"Get married, have a family, maybe work for the railroad back home," I said. "Or maybe work in television. That's a new field and there should be plenty of jobs there. How about you?"

"I got a house in Bristol," he said. "When I get home I'm going to build a porch on the back of it and sit on that porch and drink Tennessee moonshine and smile. And if anybody asks me why I'm smiling I'm going to say it's because I ain't in France."

When we reached Hill 203 we started spreading out around it. A reconnaissance patrol went out to see how it looked while everybody else double-checked their assignments. From where I was, I thought I could see the path we were supposed to secure, but I wasn't sure.

There weren't any hedgerows, but the paths were fairly narrow and twisted up the steep hill. The Jerries waited until the first platoon had climbed nearly thirty yards before they opened up.

We couldn't see them but figured they could see us. Lt. Col. Cassell got the officers together again. When Lt. Rowe came back he was pale.

"There's going to be a big push on Vire in an hour," he said. "If we don't take this hill overlooking the city it's going to be a massacre. Omaha Beach all over again. Charlie Company's going first; they're over there in that stand of woods. We're up next."

"We getting any artillery support?" a corporal asked.

"One bombing run," Lt. Rowe said. "If we're lucky."

August 9

On Hill 203. I'm exhausted and feeling sick. We didn't get the air support we wanted on the 7th and had to slug it out. Just as well, heard that a lot of men were killed when our planes dropped bombs on the wrong area near Colombelles.

August 10

We're dug in on Hill 203 over Vire. From what I can see of the city, it's pretty messed up already, and will probably be more so by the time we clear it out. Dwyer says we're on two-hour alert, not thirty-minute. I hope he told the Germans.

On the 7th, Charlie Company led the attack and got hurt pretty bad. A lot of their men were replacements, and when the guys on point were hit, the men behind them turned and headed back. According to their company commander, there was a moment of confusion, and when the shell hit there were body parts blown every-where. Awful, just awful.

When men are wounded you can smell the blood and the gases coming from them. We got the order to move out and we had to run through the smoke and the bodies of the men from Charlie Company. Men were begging for help as they lay dying, and you couldn't stop to help them. Something heavy hit about thirty yards behind me, close enough for me to feel the heat from it, and close enough for the blast to shove me forward and onto the ground.

All I could think of was the beach, being pinned against the seawall and watching guys get torn up by Jerry fire. I scrambled to my feet and flattened out against a building. Behind, I saw more bodies and the guys scrambling back to the far side of the road.

"Scotty!" It was Bobby Joe. He was trying to pull somebody out of the line of fire. I grabbed the fallen guy by the shoulder straps and we dragged him to the base of the hill as two other guys fired over us, trying to cover us while we got to safety.

On our side of the road, built into the side of the hill, was a small house and we dragged the wounded guy into it.

J. J. and a soldier I didn't know were with me. The guy was lugging an automatic rifle. He was thin and pale, with wide shoulders.

"We're cut off!" Bobby Joe said. "I hope they don't start lobbing grenades down here."

I looked out and saw a knot of bodies lying in the road. The Germans had a concentration of automatic weapons covering the road that led to the path up the hill. Bobby Joe was right: the company couldn't get across, and we couldn't get back to them without running through a hail of bullets.

"Don't leave me . . . please don't leave me," the wounded guy we had dragged in was saying. He was looking at us, searching our faces for someone to say he was going to be all right. His right side under his arm was soaked with blood, and I figured he would go into shock pretty soon.

We propped him against a wall and J. J. covered the window. I asked the guy I didn't know what his name was, and he told me it was Henderson.

"Henderson, I'm Sgt. Collins," I said. "You cover the other window, and don't get yourself framed in it."

Bobby Joe was checking the small house and came back to say that there were only three rooms.

I tried to figure out how we were going to get the wounded guy back across the road. Even though I didn't think he was going to make it, I didn't want to leave him.

The place we had run into consisted of two tiny rooms, a toilet, and a big kitchen. The first room looked like a sitting room and the second one had a small bed in it. There was a door at the back of the kitchen, and Bobby Joe covered me as I opened it. Inside there was an empty wine rack. It reminded me of a house I had seen back in Virginia.

"Bobby Joe, you ever go to Monticello?" I asked.

"No," he answered.

I had been to Monticello, Thomas Jefferson's mansion, and I remembered that the servants cooked in a big kitchen and they had an underground passage to the main house.

I was about to close the doors when Bobby Joe looked up and saw a trapdoor in the ceiling. It wasn't more than six feet up and I could reach it with a chair. I held my breath as I pushed it open. It was a dark, narrow passageway with a dim light at the top. The wooden ladder that went up one side didn't look too safe, but I knew going out the front door wasn't a good idea.

"The servants can take wine up through there if they need to," I said. "You think the Jerries know about it?" Bobby Joe asked.

I shrugged and asked J. J. what was going on outside, and he said a few guys had tried to get across the road and hadn't made it.

"They must have a concrete bunker built up there," he said.

I thought that wasn't likely.

The passageway was too narrow to get up with a pack on, so I took mine off. I told Bobby Joe to wait until I got up and gave him a signal.

I climbed onto the chair and then into the hole. I had the sling of my M-1 draped over my right hand. It would be useless while I was climbing.

Near the top I stopped to listen. I could hear the sounds of battle, but they seemed far off. Slowly I eased the rest of the way up and out of the hole into a small closet. There wasn't any noise coming from the outside of the closet, and I opened the door and found myself in a dining room. The firing was more distinct now, and I made my way to a window and eased back the curtain. There was a German machine-gun nest, made out of sandbags and what looked like the door off a truck. They were under a rock formation that gave them shelter from the air, and looked pretty cozy.

I went back to the hole and signaled for Bobby Joe and the others to come up.

It took them five minutes to get up into the house. I got Henderson to set up the automatic rifle on a table that Bobby Joe and J. J. eased up to the window.

The Germans never knew what hit them. They were protected from the fire coming up at them, but their flank was open. When we knocked out their gun, Bobby Joe went to the front window. From there he could see the whole road, and he signaled down. Some guys pointed down the side of the mountain. We went up to the next floor, and saw they were pointing to what sounded like a fifty-caliber machine gun. J. J. tossed down a grenade as me, Henderson, and Bobby Joe opened up from the windows.

Soon as we opened up, the German gun went quiet, and moments later our guys were pouring onto the mountain.

Lt. Rowe made a lot of us get into the house and up into the main house. He said he was going to make sure it made it into the battle reports. The wounded guy, the one we had dragged into the house, died before the medics could get to him.

August 11

0800. Hot food. Powdered eggs and fried Spam (from Bobby Joe) tasted as good as anything I have eaten. There are still pockets of Germans to be cleared out, but it looks good. We watched from Hill 203 as guys from the Ninth Infantry slogged through the mud headed toward Vire. They gave us the thumbs-up sign and we flashed the V for victory.

Lt. Rowe told me what Vire had cost. We lost 107 men Killed in Action, 862 Wounded in Action, 151 Missing in

Action. It was another city taken, another list of guys down, and hopefully another step toward ending the war.

August 14

We got over a thousand replacements!

"Not a good sign," Bobby Joe said.

We didn't want to see replacements; we wanted to see us going home. I went into Vire with Lt. Rowe to get some training in map reading. We were headed toward the town square and had stopped to ask directions when we came under fire. I grabbed my rifle and jumped out of the jeep to run for cover.

I thought I had banged my knee into the side of the jeep. There was an incredible pain in my leg, and it went numb as my rifle clattered to the ground. There was firing all around me, and I turned onto my stomach to get a good prone firing position. It turned out to be just sniper fire, and they flushed out two German noncoms dressed in civilian clothing from a building over a restaurant.

"Medic!" Lt. Rowe was calling out.

At first I didn't know what was wrong with him, because he looked okay, and then I realized he was calling the medics for me. I had been shot just above the knee.

There was pain. A lot of pain. But more than that I felt panicky. All of a sudden I was afraid of being left alone.

Lt. Rowe kept reassuring me, saying that I was going to be all right.

When I got to the field hospital, a doctor said I would be as good as new in a few months.

"English food is good for leg wounds," he said.

Bobby Joe came to see me. He told me that our outfit is going to get some rest and is now assigned to First United States Army Reserve.

August 16

Bobby Joe came back to say good-bye and to tell me that we are attached to the 29th again, and on the move.

"We're too good to be out of the fighting," he said. "We're headed toward Brest."

"Bobby Joe, watch your intervals," I told him. "Don't let the new guys bunch up on you."

"Hey, don't be getting soft on me," he said with a grin. "Bobby Joe ain't no rookie."

I said good-bye to him again and when I took his hand I didn't want to let it go.

August 24, Omaha Beach

I can't believe how organized the beach was. It didn't seem like the same place I landed on a little more than two months ago. There were guys unloading LSTs, mountains of equipment pouring in a steady stream up over the beach. There were also coffins, neatly stacked, with an honor guard arranged around them and an American flag flying over them. I thought about the guy we had dragged into the house at Hill 203, and about Kerlin, and Wojo, and Mikey and all the guys who had started out with me in Virginia.

I was on a stretcher with the wounded. A navy officer came and told us we would be loaded up soon. The officer, his name was McFarland, checked my dog tags against his list.

"Hey, you were wounded on your birthday!" he said.

"Yeah."

I guess he saw I was having a bad time and he asked me if I needed anything for pain. I told him no. I didn't want to tell him I was worrying about Bobby Joe and J. J. and Lt. Rowe, my guys pushing on toward Brest.

"I think the delay is because the water is so choppy," McFarland said. "They don't want the trip to be bad."

I sat up and looked out over the beach teeming with men, almost covered with equipment. Beyond the loose dirt and sand was the English Channel. I had seen it choppier.

Epilogue

✳ ✳ ✳

The 116th Infantry Regiment was made up of young Americans, many from central Virginia, who offered up their lives for a cause in which they believed. Beginning with the horrendous D-Day landing, they fought in some of the most brutal battles of World War II. Hundreds died on Omaha Beach, many without ever reaching the shore. Once onshore in Normandy, every foot of ground taken by the regiment from the determined and often desperate German army was paid for with blood.

The landing on Omaha Beach took 341 lives from the 116th. The first company to leave the boats lost close to 90 percent of its personnel, either killed or wounded.

The battle for St. Lô resulted in 87 men listed as Killed in Action, including Major Howie, 648 men Wounded in Action, and 113 men Missing in Action.

And so on it went, as the regiment moved on to Brest, and then into Holland, and finally Germany. Each city, each hamlet, would be marked by the falling of more young men. They fought in Europe until the end of the war in May and finally began the journey home by ship on Christmas Eve, 1945.

Lieutenant Arthur Rowe, wounded at Brest, opened a sporting-goods store in Roanoke and coached high school basketball for twenty-five years. He died in the Veterans' Hospital in Martinsburg, West Virginia, in June 1986.

J. J. Dandridge stayed in the army and was stationed in White Sands, New Mexico, in 1956, during the atomic bomb tests. He left the army in 1960. At loose ends in civilian life, J. J. had a series of jobs and began drinking heavily. He was homeless in 1963 and was arrested for petty theft. After his release he entered a Veterans of Foreign Wars-sponsored rehabilitation program. He met and married Ellen Custis, a nurse whose husband had been killed in the Korean War. J. J. did volunteer counseling for the Salvation Army in Roanoke until the summer of 1990, when he died of leukemia.

Bobby Joe Hunter went to William and Mary College under the GI Bill, earning a bachelor's degree in history. For thirty years he worked as a teacher in the Winchester, Virginia, school system. On retirement he and his wife, the former Sylvia Cooke, opened a used bookshop in Fredericksburg, Virginia. Each year, on Memorial Day, the Hunters, along with other area veterans, give a party for children in the local hospital.

Angie Gardiner moved with her parents to Anniston,

Alabama, in the summer of 1945, shortly before the end of the war in Europe. She wrote to Scott for a few months, but then met and married John Bryan Gadsen, a naval officer. She went with him to the San Diego Naval Station. The couple had six children. After her husband's death, Angie Gardiner Gadsen became a school crossing guard. She still lives in San Diego.

Scott Pendleton Collins came back to Roanoke after the war and lived with his parents. The wounds he received in Vire left him with a permanent limp. He started college under the GI Bill, but dropped out after a year to work. He found a job as a short-order cook in a restaurant, where he met Julia Bennett. They were married in 1952 and had three children: Nancy, Joseph, and Michael Collins.

Scott kept in touch with J. J. Dandridge for a while but then lost contact with him when he and Julia opened their own restaurant in Christianburg. The restaurant was successful, but Scott, whose wounded leg was amputated in 1973, had to retire early. He spent the rest of his life working with troubled youngsters in the Roanoke area.

Scott's son Joseph, a pilot, was killed in aerial combat in Vietnam in 1968, during the Tet Offensive. Nancy runs the restaurant and Michael is a minister in Duluth, Minnesota.

Scott and Julia stayed in touch with his best friend,

Bobby Joe Hunter, and his wife for the remainder of their lives.

Scott Pendleton Collins died on March 19, 1992, at the age of 65. Julia now lives in a small apartment just outside Roanoke. The house she had lived in is being used as a group home for youngsters. In the living room over the couch, there are four pictures. Besides the two pictures of Scott's great-grandfather and father, there is also a picture of Scott Pendleton Collins and one of his sons, Joseph.

The central player in this story is the war itself. It lives on.

Life in America
in 1944

Historical Note

✳ ✳ ✳

The events leading to the invasion of Normandy began at the end of the First World War. Germany, defeated on the battlefield and forced to sign a humiliating peace treaty, was in a state of confusion. German currency was practically worthless and many people were close to starvation. Thousands of jobless veterans roamed the streets, feeling betrayed by their government and looking for some way to redeem themselves. These conditions, bordering on social and political chaos, created a unique opportunity for anyone shrewd enough and ruthless enough to take advantage of them. Such a person was Adolf Hitler.

Hitler was born in Austria, on April 20, 1889. As a young man he studied art, but was not successful in his wish to become an architect. He fought in World War I, and after the war became involved in the *Nationalsozialistische Deutsche Arbeiterpartei*, popularly known as the Nazi party.

The late twenties and early thirties were the years of a global economic depression. In the United States, a man named Franklin Roosevelt promised, with hard work and government help, to bring America out of the Depression. In Germany, Adolf Hitler built up the Nazi party with promises to bring his nation to a position of worldwide dominance. The German people, anxious to at last escape the crippling depression, first tolerated this charismatic man, but then grew to fear him. Hitler surrounded himself with men who were loyal and as willing to use terror and violence to achieve their ends as Hitler was. Hitler's vision was of a master race expanding to fulfill what he considered to be the destiny of the German people.

One way of establishing power is to create a strong and loyal army. Hitler worked hard to build such an army even as he worked to create the myth of himself as a superman sent to lead his people to greatness. Part of his idea of the pureness of the German race required the extermination of what he considered to be non-pure people, such as Jews, Gypsies, homosexuals, and non-whites.

By 1938, Hitler felt ready to begin his quest for world domination. He began to claim territories that he announced as being German in character. German armies rolled into Austria and occupied large areas without firing a shot. In 1939, Hitler's armies occupied Czechoslovakia and Poland, killing thousands of civilians while overwhelming the armies of those countries. It was clear to the rest of the world that Hitler and the Nazis were intending to dominate, by force, all of Europe.

France and England declared war against Germany, but a confident Hitler moved on, ordering his armies first into Denmark and Norway, and then France. By the end of June 1940, the Germans' *blitzkrieg*, the lightning attacks of planes and armored vehicles used by the German army, had forced the French to submit to a peace treaty.

England presented a different problem to the aggressive Nazi army. Bringing an army across the natural barrier of the English Channel depended on essentially subduing the British by air attacks. In the fall of 1940 the Battle of Britain began with German bombers invading England. But British fighters and antiaircraft guns, more sophisticated than any the Germans had faced before, exacted a heavy toll on the German bombers. The British people, although badly shaken by the destruction from the skies, had the resolve to withstand the bombing. They would not surrender.

Winston Churchill, the prime minister of Great Britain, appealed to the United States for funds and material to fight off the Nazi aggression. Roosevelt agreed to the request and tons of equipment began to cross the Atlantic. German submarines sank some American ships but enough got through to help England fight back. Then, on a bright Sunday morning, December 7,

1941, the Japanese attacked Pearl Harbor, an American naval base in Hawaii. Thousands were killed in this vicious raid by a Japanese war machine intent on expanding its small island territory in the Pacific. Two days later, Germany, which was allied with Japan, declared war on the United States.

Hitler, his confidence bolstered by his victories in Europe, thought it was just a matter of time before he would be capable of launching a successful attack on England. His vision of world domination seemed within his grasp. But he had made mistakes that would cost him dearly.

Hitler badly underestimated the ability of the United States to produce war materials that would equal those of Germany. He occupied France but he needed time to build the ships and boats required for an attack across the English Channel. By 1944, American bombers, flying from bases in North Africa, were bombing German cities. On the eastern front the Russians were taking back their cities. In England, there was a great buildup of English and American troops. The Germans knew these troops were meant to be an invasion force.

Thousands of men were being drafted to fight in the war. National Guard units were activated, and thousands of men and women volunteered to help rid the world of Nazi aggression in Europe and Japanese war-making in the Far East.

The Germans knew the invasion of France was coming. A leading German general, field marshal Erwin Rommel, had supervised the building of the defenses along the coasts of France. They seemed virtually impregnable. The English and Americans, led by American general Dwight D. Eisenhower and field marshal Bernard Law Montgomery, who was Commander-in-Chief, Ground Forces, understood the price in human lives that would be paid by the invasion. But the evil that Hitler represented had to be destroyed. On D-Day, June 6, 1944, the beginning of that effort began with the landings in Normandy.

The battle of Normandy was difficult. It took weeks against a determined Nazi army for the Americans and British to break out of the Normandy area. But break out they did, in battles at places such as Saint-Lô, Vire, Cherbourg, Brest, and the Ardennes. The invasion found men who would become heroes, and heroes who would save the world.

Hitler, the man responsible for the deaths through warfare of millions of soldiers and civilians, as well as the planned deaths of millions of Jews, Gypsies, homosexuals, and other political enemies of the Nazis, committed suicide in April, 1945.

Dwight Eisenhower, a four-star general in the U.S. Army, was the Supreme Commander of Operation Overlord, the Allied assault on Nazi-occupied western Europe. On June 5, 1944, three days before the invasion would take place, Eisenhower talks to the 101st Airborne, stationed in England.

On D-Day, when Operation Overlord was set in motion, Eisenhower commanded 39 land assault divisions, each with approximately 20,000 troops, 5,000 ships and smaller craft, and 50,000 vehicles, with 11,000 aircraft overhead. When American troops hit the beaches of Normandy on June 6, 1944, they faced obstacles in the surf, land mines, barbed wire, antitank ditches, and a barrage of fire from German guns.

The Nazi troops erected their fortifications against the Allied forces' attack long before D-Day. These obstacles were veiled at high tide, imperiling ships and landing craft; they forced the Allies to land at low tide, when the killing zone was at its greatest. Along with the casualties in the foreground are several Allied vehicles destroyed during the attack.

After scrambling across the beach, these troops sought protection behind a concrete wall. In the center and lower right corner, a censor has blotted out the regiment's insignia on the left shoulder of two soldiers' uniforms.

As D-Day wore on, many soldiers were killed, wounded, or captured. This group of wounded American assault troops sought the safety of a bluff after storming Omaha Beach. A total of 675,000 American soldiers were wounded in World War II, and 292,000 were killed or missing in action.

After his landing craft is sunk off the coast of Normandy on D-Day, a wounded U.S. soldier receives a plasma transfusion.

Red Army Expected to Launch General Offensive in East Before Week End

Weather

The Roanoke World-News ★ ★

VOL. 83—No. 135 —18 PAGES— ROANOKE, VIRGINIA, TUESDAY AFTERNOON, JUNE 6, 1944 TWO SECTIONS PRICE FIVE CENTS

Allied Forces Plunge Into France, Drive Nine Miles Inland; Troops Ram Through Nazi Lines Against Slight Opposition; 4,000 Transports Ferry Great Expeditionary Army Over Channel

11,000 Warplanes Blast Path Into Hitler's Fortress

Bombers, Fighters Pound Inland Communications

By W. W. HERCHER

Mighty Assault by Land, Sea and Air Crumples Nazi Defenses in Normandy; Losses Reported Less than Anticipated

600 Naval Guns Throw 2,000 Tons Of Shells at Nazis Every 10 Minutes

By PIERRE HUSS

Airborne Forces Fighting In the Streets of Caen

By WES GALLAGHER

The Roanoke World-News announces the Allied forces' landing at Normandy. Though the headline indicates that there was only slight opposition, casualties among the first wave of troops to arrive were horrendous, and the success of the landing was in doubt for several hours.

Allied forces are amassed offshore at Omaha Beach as support equipment is unloaded. Backing up the initial troops who landed at Normandy were almost three million troops who assembled in England before the invasion. Barrage balloons were anchored to many ships to discourage low-flying enemy planes.

The U.S. Army Air Force dropped men and supplies over a new beachhead as part of Operation Uppercut. *Above, parachutes fill the sky over southern France, somewhere between Nice and Marseilles.*

Adolf Hitler, leader of the Nazi Party, salutes his troops. Hitler became Chancellor of the Reich in January 1933, inaugurating a reign of violence that lasted for twelve years. Within three months of his taking power, all German clubs for boys and girls between the ages of ten and eighteen were consolidated into the Hitler Youth, which had a membership of 8.9 million when war came in 1939.

In 1937, the first year of the Hitler Youth's rifle school, more than 1.5 million boys were taught to shoot. Here, a young German soldier surrenders. He is wearing an Iron Cross, one of many medals and insignia meant to enhance the self-esteem and sense of authority of the Nazi Party.

Sherman tanks were an important part of the Allied invasion force. The Sherman had a motor designed to run for three thousand miles without a major overhaul and was known for its durability in the throes of war. Here, a Sherman tank rumbles through the ruins of Flere, France, in August of 1944.

St. Lô, France, was demolished during the Normandy Invasion. Above, U.S. soldiers patrol the ruins of St. Lô on July 25, 1944. In the background is the Notre Dame Cathedral.

An American soldier adjusts the elevation of a mortar, a short-barreled cannon used to hurl shells at the enemy. Germany suffered more than six million civilian and military casualties during and immediately after World War II.

The battle-wise Infantryman...

...is **CAREFUL** of what he says or writes

HOW ABOUT YOU?

Soldiers' letters to friends and family were closely monitored by censors in order to maintain secrecy about the invasion and subsequent movements. This World War II poster emphasizes the importance of using discretion in regard to dates and troop locations.

A French girl presents flowers to members of an American tank crew in appreciation for the liberation of the town of Avranches, France. As they made their way farther and farther into Europe, American soldiers often mingled with European civilians, who were thankful for the Allied forces' presence.

Since Nazi attacks were unpredictable, soldiers had to grab a bite to eat whenever they could. Above, three American soldiers down their rations in a foxhole in Normandy, France.

The hedgerows in Normandy provided protection for the German soldiers defending the area, but Allied forces took advantage of them as well. Here, a line of 411th Infantrymen of the U.S. Seventh Army take positions along a hedgerow in Alsace, France. Geese wander by, seemingly unaware of the danger that surrounds them.

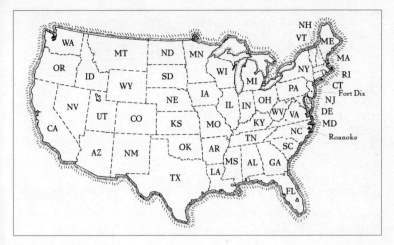

Modern map of the United States, showing the locations of Roanoke, Virginia, and Fort Dix, New Jersey.

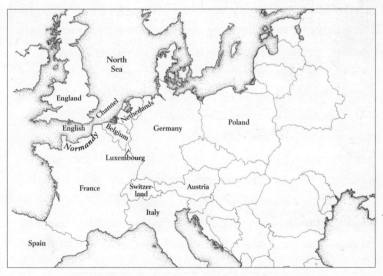

Map of Western Europe, showing the location of Normandy.

About the Author

✶ ✶ ✶

Walter Dean Myers says, "There is no more dramatic event in a country's history than the occurrence of a war. We have a tendency to talk about war in larger than life terms — invasions, battle plans, and grand campaigns. But all wars, in my mind, depend ultimately on individual soldiers like Scotty. Talk about 'smart bombs' and 'saturation bombing' tends to let us forget about the families of the soldiers, the dreams, beliefs, and aspirations which personalize the sacrifices endured. It's important to me to write about this intensely personal concept of war. The losses suffered on D-Day and during all of the war should be remembered forever and should always be a restraint when we think about military actions to solve international problems. I can think of no better way to prevent war than to present a true picture of its horrors."

Walter Dean Myers is an award-winning writer of fiction, nonfiction, and poetry for young people. His many books include *The Journal of Joshua Loper, A Black Cowboy*, in the My Name Is America series; *Slam!*; *Somewhere in the Darkness; Fallen Angels,* winner of the Coretta Scott King Award; *Malcolm X: By Any Means Necessary,* a Coretta Scott King Honor Book and ALA Notable Children's Book; and *The Glory Field,* an ALA Best Book for Young Adults and a Notable Children's Trade Book in the Field of Social Studies. Mr. Myers is the recipient of two awards for the body of his work: the Margaret A. Edwards Award for Outstanding Literature for Young Adults and the ALAN Award. He lives in Jersey City, New Jersey.

For Nancy Larrick,
whose concerns helped bring me into
the field of children's literature

Acknowledgments

❋ ❋ ❋

The author would like to thank Henry B. McFarland, a naval officer during the war, who shared his experiences of the Normandy Invasion, and Joan Trew of the Roanoke City Library for her help in background research.

Grateful acknowledgment is made for permission to reprint the following:

Cover portrait: Photograph of soldier, Culver Pictures.

Cover background: Photograph of U.S. troops landing at Normandy, France, National Archives.

"Don't Sit Under the Apple Tree" by Lou Brown, Sam Stept, and Charles Tobias. Published by EMI/Robbins and Shed Music. All rights reserved.

Page 124 (top): Dwight Eisenhower, National Archives.
Page 124 (bottom): Troops landing at Normandy, France, ibid.
Page 125 (top): Obstacles, AP/Wide World Photos.
Page 125 (bottom): Troops at seawall, UPI/Corbis.
Page 126: Wounded soldiers, National Archives.

Page 126: Wounded soldiers, National Archives.

Page 127 (top): Soldier receiving medical care, Archive Photos.

Page 127 (bottom): *The Roanoke World-News*.

Page 128: Barrage balloons, National Archives.

Page 129: Paratroopers, AP/Wide World Photos.

Page 130 (top): Adolf Hitler, Archive Photos.

Page 130 (bottom): German soldier, The Trustees of the Imperial War Museum, London.

Page 131 (top): Sherman tank, Archive Photos.

Page 131 (bottom): St. Lô, ibid.

Page 132: Soldier with mortar, ibid.

Page 133 (top): *Battle-Wise Infantryman*, West Point Museum Collection, United States Military Academy.

Page 133 (bottom): French girl, AP/Wide World Photos.

Page 134 (top): Soldiers in foxhole, ibid.

Page 134 (bottom): Soldiers behind hedgerows, ibid.

Page 135: Maps by Heather Saunders.

Other books in the My Name Is America series

✳ ✳ ✳

The Journal of William Thomas Emerson
A Revolutionary War Patriot
by Barry Denenberg

The Journal of James Edmond Pease
A Civil War Union Soldier
by Jim Murphy

The Journal of Joshua Loper
A Black Cowboy
by Walter Dean Myers

All rights reserved. Published by Scholastic Inc.
SCHOLASTIC, MY NAME IS AMERICA, and associated logos are trademarks and/or registered trademarks of Scholastic Inc.

ISBN-13: 978-0-545-05066-1
ISBN-10: 0-545-05066-9

12 11 10 9 8 7 6 5 4 3 2   7 8 9 10 11/0

Printed in the U.S.A.   40

This edition first printing, September 2007

The display type was set in Old Typewriter Regular.
The text type was set in Berling.
Book design by Elizabeth B. Parisi
Photo research by Zoe Moffitt

✻ ✻ ✻